LSTs:
The Ships with
the BIG MOUTH

Om best wishes,

Homer Heswell

one of—
the original
writers ships
'ern

LSTs:
The Ships with the
BIG MOUTH

HOMER HASWELL

The History and Adventures of LST 698
(Landing Ship Tank) and What Made
These Ships So Essential in Island
Actions of World War II (1944-45)

To order additional copies of this book, contact:
Xlibris Corporation
1-888-795-4274
www.Xlibris.com
Orders@Xlibris.com
24945

Contents

Maps and Charts ix

Acknowledgements xi

Permissions to Use Copyrighted Materials xiii

Preface: Suddenly We Were in a New Kind of War xix

Introduction: Putting America's
    Huge Resources to Work xxiii

1 Parting Is Tough 1
2 Fitting Her Out and Shaking Her Down 4
3 It Wasn't JUST Pearl Harbor; How Japanese Attacks
    Brought U.S. into the War 8
4 First Western Pacific Allied Footholds 13
5 The Blue Caribbean Beckons, Threatens 19
6 Panama Canal, Shortcut to Pacific 24
7 Guitars, Infantry, Drills off Maui 29
8 Hundreds of Ships—All Going to Yap? 34
9 Strategy Changes—Timetable Moves Up 38
10 Third Wave at Leyte; 3 Busy Days 43
11 The Naval Battle for Leyte Gulf 55
12 Quiet Interlude, Sailing to Hollandia 58
13 We Explore Humboldt Bay 63
14 We Carry Air Force Troops to Leyte 66
15 Hard Work—and Little "Meatball" 71
16 Eight Men in a Boat—Learning 74
17 We Take on Medics, Ambulances 78

18 What a Time for an Appendectomy! 82
19 On Morotai, a Tropical Christmas 85
20 Frantic Search for a 1945 Almanac 89
21 Bridge-Builders Invade Luzon 94
22 A Vital Lesson in Navigation 102
23 Tacloban, a Different Kind of Base 107
24 A Little Mail, Ten Tons of Meat 111
25 Guadalcanal—and It's a BOY! 117
26 A Radio That's Just for Listening 123
27 Busy Seabees Head for Okinawa..................... 125
28 Where in the World Is Ulithi? 128
29 In Kerama Retto without a Chart 133
30 How We Wrecked Our Ship................... 140
31 President Roosevelt Dies............................... 152
32 At Ulithi, We Await Our Fate 155
33 What Happened to the LST 884?..................... 162
34 The Cable Snaps! We're Adrift! 166
35 Tedium Turns to Jubilation 171
36 Hawaii—A Glorious Return! 178
37 To Portland, and THE WAR ENDS 185
38 One Era Ends, Another Begins..................... 195
39 Reflections: the War, the Navy, the Bomb 199

Appendices:
Where to See an LST 204
LST Associations 205
LST Shipyard Museum 206
Where the LSTs Were Built................................ 206
Itinerary—U.S.S. LST 698, 1944-1945 207
Passengers and Cargo Carried.......................... 212
Shipmates : The Men Who Ran the LST 698................ 214
Report of Damage to U.S.S. LST 698.......................... 220
Information Sources 222
About the Author 230
Index of Places (World War II Names) 232

Dedication

First to my wife, Frances Ellis Haswell. She is the Fran I refer to throughout the book, whom I had to leave in June 1944 (Chapter 1) to board the *LST 698* and to whom I returned 15 months later, to share the rest of our lives together. In 2004 we celebrated our 62nd anniversary.

Second, to our children. The arrival of our first son, William Ellis Haswell, Evanston, Ill., was recorded in Chapter 25. He was followed, after I returned home, by Anne Marinello, Woodstock, Vt., Clayton Haswell, Walnut Creek, Calif., and James Haswell, Madison, Wis.

Finally, to our grandchildren, Brent, Heather, and Kyle Marinello; Sam Haswell; and Emily and a second Sam Haswell.

A truck emerges over the bow ramp of LST 700 at Tacloban, Philippines, and onto an earthen causeway to shore. Earlier, a few miles south, our LST had carried infantry to Dulag and in the third wave released them in amphibious tractors and LCVPs. *National Archives.*

Maps and Charts

Maps: The World War II Odyssey of U.S.S. LST 698 . . .
(Western Pacific and Eastern Pacific) xvi

Chart: Leyte Gulf 46

Map: Philippine Travels 97

Chart: Lingayen Gulf 100

Map: Activities in the Western Pacific 129

Chart: Okinawa Gunto (showing Kerama Retto) 137

Chart: Okinawa Beaches 143

Map: We Travel 7,100 Miles under Tow 159

Acknowledgements

Many folks contributed in a variety of ways to this book. Foremost is my wife Fran, who was with me every day yet half a world away. She wrote letters to me daily and also stored the letters I wrote to her while I was overseas. My letters turned out to be a record of hundreds of happenings aboard our *LST 698*—in one sense, a partial framework for the book.

My children read the manuscript and offered suggestions and encouragement along the way, as did some of my friends who learned of my project.

The National Archives provided me with daily logs of our ship, action reports, and numerous photographs. These photos were supplemented by some from Real War Photos, Hammond, Ind., and a few from our shipmates, which were made after our return to Pearl Harbor. (We could not take pictures in the war zones.)

On some points, I sent out informal queries to fellow *698* officers. I obtained some wonderful responses—from Al Toll, Bill Chapman, Ralph Hart, Bruce Montgomery, Angelo Prezioso, and the late Ed Erickson.

For historic details of the war itself, I dug into scores of books as revealed in "Sources" at the back of the book, with particular thanks to those who gave me permission to print direct quotations from them. (See "Permissions")

DeVere Appleyard prepared the maps, and Sherri Nichols took the photo of me that's on the back cover. The late Allen Carr offered design ideas in the early stages of the book. Carmela Farolan provided the technological and editing skills in pulling it all together.

Thank you all!

Permissions to Use Copyrighted Materials

I saw the war from the vantage point of the *U.S.S. LST 698*. But many actions and decisions occurred elsewhere, perhaps thousands of miles away, which had an effect upon our actions and our lives.

For events involving our own ship I had such resources as our ship's deck logs, war diaries, and action reports, all available from the National Archives. And I had the letters to my wife Fran, which she had saved.

But now, almost 60 years later, hundreds of books have been written about various aspects of World War II, and I have utilized information from some of these writings to help the reader put my story in better perspective. (See "Sources" at the back of the book.)

Besides noting the sources in my endnotes, I obtained written permission to reproduce occasional quotations in accordance with federal copyright laws. I am grateful particularly to the writers below and their publishers for permission to use their words:

Joseph A. Alexander, *Storm Landings: Epic Amphibious Battles in the Central Pacific,* Naval Institute Press, 1997. (Comments on LSTs and Okinawa invasion)

Vice Admiral Daniel E. Barbey, *MacArthur's Amphibious Navy,* Naval Institute Press, 1969. (Early Southwest Pacific amphibious operations)

Harry A. Gailey, *The War in the Pacific, from Pearl Harbor to Tokyo Bay,* copyright 1995, Presidio Press. Permission granted by Random

House, Inc. (Analysis of Pearl Harbor assault and battle of Midway)

Jeter A. Isely and Philip A. Crowl, *The U.S. Marines and Amphibious War,* Princeton University Press, 1951. (Okinawa and LSTs)

Capt. Walter Karig, USNR, Lt. Cdr. Russell L. Harris, USNR, and Lt. Cdr. Frank A. Manson, USN, *Battle Report: Victory in the Pacific,* copyright 1949, Rinehart & Company, Inc. Reprinted by permission of Henry Holt & Co., LLC. (Plan proposed for 1945 assault on Japanese mainland)

David McCullough, *The Path between the Seas,* copyright 1977, David McCullough. Reprinted with permission of Simon & Schuster Adult Publishing Group. (Panama Canal)

Henri Michel, *The Second World War,* copyright 1975, Praeger Publishers. Permission from Greenwood Publishing Group, Inc. (Early Japanese strikes)

Samuel Eliot Morison, *The Two-Ocean War,* Little, Brown and Company,1963. Also pertinent portions of Morison's 15-volume *History of U.S. Naval Operations in World War II* (also Little, Brown*),* particularly*: Vol. V: Struggle for Guadalcanal, August 1942-February 1943,* 1949; *Vol. XII: Leyte, June 1944-January 1945,* 1958*; and Vol. XIV: Victory in the Pacific, 1945,* 1975. (Amphibious operations using LSTs; Guadalcanal; Leyte Gulf; Battle for Leyte Gulf; Lingayen Gulf; Okinawa)

Williamson Murray and Allan R. Millett, *A War to Be Won: Fighting the Second World War,* The Belknap Press of Harvard University Press, Cambridge, Mass., copyright 2000 by "President and Fellows of Harvard College." Reprinted by permission of the publishers. (American losses at Okinawa)

Norman Polmar and Thomas B. Allen, *World War II, America at War,* copyright 1991, Random House, Inc. (Churchill on LSTs)

C. Vann Woodward, *Battle for Leyte Gulf,* copyright 1947, The Macmillan Company. Permission from Simon & Schuster. (Great naval battle following Leyte invasion)

Col. Hiromichi Yahara, *Battle for Okinawa,* copyright 1995, Pacific Basin

Institute. This material is used with permission of John Wiley &
Sons, Inc. (Okinawa as viewed from the Japanese perspective)

Thank you!

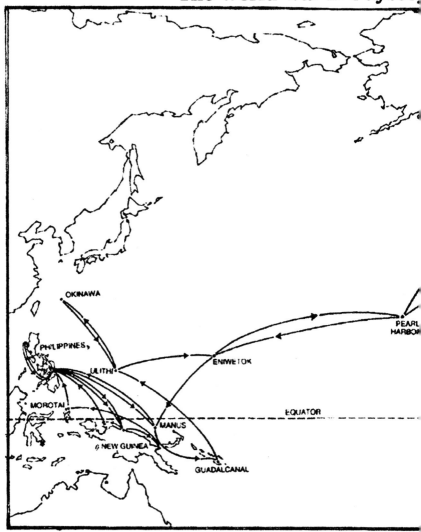

Distances are vast in the Pacific. We traveled some 5,070 miles from Pearl Harbor to our first encounter, Leyte, in the Philippines.

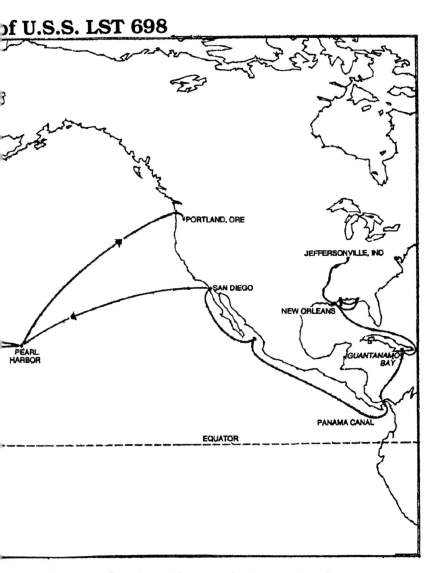

Our voyage from New Orleans to the Panama Canal to San Diego to Pearl Harbor was roughly 4,470 miles. Returning home under tow from Okinawa via Ulithi, Eniwetok, and Pearl Harbor to Portland, Ore., was about 7,190 miles.

Preface

Suddenly We Were in a
New Kind of War

*LSTs (landing ships tank) of the Amphibious Forces
were designed to charge bow-first right up onto the beach to
discharge their cargo (or pick it up) through doors in their
bow, at great savings in time*

During the three years after the keel of the first LST was laid in
June 1942, over a thousand of these strange ships were turned out.
Each was staffed by up to 130 men and a dozen officers, most of whom
had boarded a ship for the first time when they attended amphibious
school on Chesapeake Bay.

These pages portray what life was like aboard one such LST. It is a
history of *U.S.S. LST 698* from its commissioning in New Orleans on 3
June 1944 to its joyful return to mainland United States at Portland,
Ore., on 14 August 1945, the day the war ended. The ship participated
in the three largest amphibious assaults in the Pacific—Leyte Gulf
and Lingayen Gulf in the Philippines, and Okinawa. It visited such
islands as New Guinea, Biak, Manus, Guadalcanal, Tulagi, and Morotai,
places where history had been made before we got there.

LST 698 traveled some 31,400 nautical miles (36,130 statute miles), roughly 1.45 times the circumference of the earth. But after the ship was disabled on a coral reef off Okinawa, we were *towed* for the last 7,190 miles—back to Ulithi, Eniwetok, Pearl Harbor, and finally to Portland, Ore.

Ships like ours became a major part of the armadas of amphibious forces that brought the men, vehicles, and supplies to those little-known islands of the Pacific.

An LST like ours operated like a complete city. Men had been trained in amphibious school not only in the standard seaman tasks but in such specialties as electricity, refrigeration, welding, radio, radar, or the gyrocompass. They also had what was often known as "horse sense." The crew never knew when they would be called upon to fix something or to take on an unusual assignment.

When the chips were down, these men combined newly acquired seamanship knowledge with Yankee ingenuity. They may have started out pretty green, but they learned the ropes in a hurry. They became resourceful and developed confidence in themselves in ways they had never expected. They performed uncommonly well in the jobs they were assigned to do.

*   *   *

Facts of major events like invasions are based on our LST ship logs, navigational charts, official reports, and the books of naval history. But most of the reports of day-to-day happenings on our LST came from letters I wrote some 60 years ago to my wife Fran. Because of censorship, I could never mention place names, ship names, or military events in my letters, and nothing at all about the invasions until cleared to do so a month or two afterward.

What follows is a true story, sometimes tense, sometimes light-hearted, of happenings aboard *LST 698*, woven into their historic context. The events are real; so are the names. And the stories show how quickly these young men adapted to their new seaborne environment.

Homer Haswell

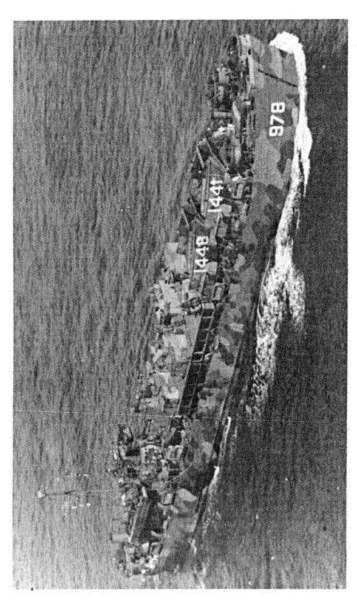

One of 1,051 LSTs (landing ships tank) built in World War II to charge bow-first right up to the shore to discharge or take on personnel, vehicles and practically all kinds of supplies in places where there were no docks. *Real War Photos.*

Introduction

Putting America's
Huge Resources to Work

The Pacific War focused on amphibious warfare. Strange new ships came into the thick of it. In January 1942 the LST (Landing Ship Tank) had still been on the drawing board, but by the end of the war 1,051 had been produced; it proved outstandingly successful

A great sense of urgency came over Washington in the days following Pearl Harbor. It was promptly determined that the war in the Pacific would be like no other war before. Distances were vast. Most of those islands had no docks for loading or unloading. The need was immense for ships that could carry troops right up to the beaches, rather than to the customary piers.

But *could* a ship carry men and vehicles and supplies directly to the shore without first transferring them to boats? The LST (landing ship tank) was designed and built with exactly that in mind. Other ships built with similar intent included the LSM (landing ship medium) and the LSI (landing ship infantry).

The arrival of the first LSTs and other amphibious vessels in 1943 drastically changed the complexion of fighting in the Pacific. "More territory would be gained in a few weeks than had been gained in the previous 12 months," according to Vice Admiral Daniel E. Barbey, USN (Ret.) "All this was made possible by the new ships and the new men of the new amphibious Navy."[1]

The LST became the backbone of the amphibious force. Historians Norman Polmar and Thomas B. Allen considered it "probably the most important ship in the Allied war effort."[2] In 1944 Prime Minister Churchill declared:

> The whole of this difficult [strategy] question only arises out of the absurd shortage of the LSTs. How is it that the plans of two great empires like Britain and the United States should be so much hamstrung and limited by a hundred or two of the particular vessels will never be understood by history.[3]

What was unique about the LSTs? And why were they so widely needed? Here's what they could do:

On signal from the beachmaster, our LST charged at flank speed toward the beach. When conditions were right, we were able to put the bow 10 to 20 feet up onto the sandy shore. To hold our position, thousands of gallons of ballast were pumped forward into tanks near the bow.

The bow doors opened and a huge bow ramp, which provided a strong seal when in its vertical, closed position, dropped down onto the beach. A bulldozer rumbled over the ramp and onto the beach, smoothing the earth and packing it down to make a road from our ramp. If the LST had not quite reached the shore, a few strokes of the bulldozer blade would build a road out to meet us.

In minutes we were unloading a stream of vehicles from tank deck or main deck onto shore. Front-end loaders would carry out such diverse cargo as the prebuilt parts of Quonset huts, prefabricated bridges, or TNT.

This resulted in enormous savings in unloading time, compared with transferring cargo from an offshore ship into small boats to carry it all, boatload after boatload, to the beach.

In the part of the world where docks were scarce, the concept made it possible to load ships rapidly, travel to the assault area, and then unload them just as fast at the portion of a beach strategically suited for the campaign. This is one reason our troops could move so quickly from island to island as the war progressed.

The LST's large ballast control system had a very important dual roll. It could be filled for ocean passage and then pumped out for beaching operations. After beaching, the system pumped fuel, fresh water, and seawater into forward tanks to hold the ship firmly on the beach. For withdrawing from the beach, the seawater was pumped out and the fresh water and fuel were pumped aft.

A stern anchor, dropped as the ship approached the beach, tended to hold the ship perpendicular to the shoreline. A strain taken on it aided the ship in withdrawing from the beach.

*   *   *

The need for such vehicles was first expressed after the British evacuation of Dunkirk in 1940. But with emphasis on the war in Europe, little interest in such vessels was shown until mid-1941, when the British Admiralty began conducting meetings with the U. S. Navy's Bureau of Ships.

The Bureau of Ships undertook to create a completely new ship. John C. Niedermair was credited for its actual design, according to Melvin D. Barger in *Large Slow Target, Vol. II,* a publication of the U.S. LST Association. Niedermair's first sketch "opened the era of large-ship amphibious operations," Barger said, quoting *Proceedings,* U. S. Naval Institute, 1982.[1]

Final plans, approved in January and February 1942, called for an overall length of 328 feet and a 50-foot beam. The first LST keel was laid down at Newport News, Va., on 10 June 1942. The urgent need for LSTs resulted in a high priority for them throughout the war. By war's end, 1,051 had been built.

The LSTs were 328 feet long, with 50-foot beam. Beneath the main deck was the cavernous tank deck, 288 feet long, 30 feet wide. The superstructure, aft, housed galley, mess hall and officers' quarters, and above it, navigation deck and bridge, wheelhouse and conning tower. *Real War Photos.*

Most coastal shipyards were already operating at full capacity, building large, deep-draft ships. Thus new construction facilities for LSTs had to be established along inland waterways. According to the *Dictionary of American Fighting Ships,* Vol. 7, edited by James L. Mooney, "In some instances, heavy-industry plants such as steel-fabricating yards were converted for LST construction . . . The success of these 'cornfield' shipyards of the Middle West was a revelation to the long-established shipbuilders on the coasts. Their contribution to the LST building program was enormous. Of the 1,051 LSTs built during World War II, 670 were constructed by five major inland builders."[5]

It's hard to believe the speed with which construction of LSTs got under way. Once the final design was determined, the Bureau of Ships called in the private firm of Gibbs and Cox as the Navy's central design agent, according to Barger in his *Large Slow Target.* This firm, in turn, selected Dravo Corporation to work out standardized methods of construction. The shipyards were divided into as many as 30 berths in order to work simultaneously on numerous ships at various levels of completion. Transfer carriages moved the hulls from one berth to another.[6]

A 54-hour week was common, but it sometimes ran as high as 70 hours. Much of the labor was welding, and many of the workers were women.

The Seneca, Ill., plant of Chicago Bridge and Iron, southwest of Chicago on the Illinois River, was typical. It occupied 200 acres and in 1944 employed 10,600 workers. (The town itself had a population of about 2,100.) According to Barger: "Beginning with the launching of *LST 197* on 13 December 1942, Seneca's workers turned out from four to six ships a month until the launching of the final Seneca ship, *LST 1152,* on 8 June 1945."[7] Its total of 157 was just under the top producer, Missouri Valley Bridge and Iron in Evansville, Ind., which produced 167.

Historian Samuel Eliot Morison later reported that these "handy, ubiquitous and greatly wanted"[8] LSTs had become "the handymen of the Navy." He noted, "Besides their primary employment for lifting tanks and amphtracs [amphibious tractors], LSTs had proved capable of discharging assault cargo much more rapidly than the big transports, and without transfer to landing craft. They could be used for general or specialized cargo, or specially equipped as hospital ships."[9]

Marine historian Joseph H. Alexander noted:

> The ungainly, shallow-draft, flat-bottomed LSTs may have had British origins, but in their down-home utility and versatility these ships had Made in America stamped all over them. They rode rougher than a cob, but they could beach themselves, open bow doors, lower a ramp, and discharge wheeled or tracked vehicles in shallow water or onto a causeway . . . If nothing else, the LST's shallow draft (3'4" forward, 9'6" aft in landing configuration) permitted a much closer approach to any beach, thereby greatly reducing the turnaround time for boats extracting casualties from the fight and receiving more combat cargo to return ashore.[10]

Many of the first LSTs commissioned went to Europe. But soon more and more were heading for the Pacific. They carried troops onto Guadalcanal in November 1943.

On D-Day (6 June 1944) LSTs brought 41,035 wounded men back across the English Channel from the Normandy beaches.[11] A number of LSTs were converted to landing craft repair ships (ARL).

The *Dictionary of American Naval Fighting Ships* noted:

> Throughout the war, the LSTs demonstrated a remarkable capacity to absorb punishment and survive . . . The LSTs suffered few losses in proportion to their number and the scope of their operations. Their brilliantly conceived structural arrangement provided unusual strength and buoyancy. Although the LST was considered a valuable target by the enemy, only 26 were lost due to enemy action, and a mere 13 were the victims of weather, reef or accident.[12]

Every inch of this LSTs main deck and cavernous tank deck carried vehicles, supplies and equipment. In minutes after this LST hit the beach, these trucks and jeeps rolled down the truck ramp and out the bow doors onto dry land. *National Archives.*

An outstanding design characteristic was the huge "tank deck" beneath the main deck. It was roughly 288 feet long and 30 feet wide, capable of taking on 20 tanks or some 1,900 tons of almost any combination of vehicles and cargo. A second ramp could be lowered from the main deck to permit loading or unloading of vehicles on the main deck through the bow. Earlier models had an elevator instead of a second ramp, a slower procedure.

Other design features of the LSTs: The engine room was below the after end of the tank deck. Watertight compartments for fuel, drinking water, and salt-water ballast were located throughout the ship. The superstructure on the after third of the ship housed the officers' quarters forward and the galley and mess hall in the stern. Crew's quarters were below the galley and mess hall and in three-tiered bunks in compartments along each side of the ship. The navigation bridge, above officers' country, housed the helm, the navigator's chart house, radar equipment, and the radio shack. Aft of these was the signal bridge.

Most LSTs had two LCVPs (landing craft vehicle, personnel) mounted on davits on either side aft. Our *LST 698* had six LCVPs, two forward and four aft, necessitating a higher conning tower (or conn) for better visibility. This permitted a sea cabin beneath it for the captain.

Our *LST 698* was built by the Jeffersonville Boat and Machine Company, Jeffersonville, Ind. The keel was laid down on 14 March 1944. It was launched on 5 May and commissioned on 3 June.[13]

With the hoisting of that commissioning pennant, the *U.S.S. LST 698* and her officers and crew began their role in World War II together. Who knew where it would lead them?

Notes

[1] Barbey, Daniel E., Vice Admiral USN (Ret.): *MacArthur's Amphibious Navy— Seventh Amphibious Force Operations 1943-1945,* Naval Institute Press, Annapolis, 1969, ix

[2] Polmar, Norman, and Thomas B. Allen: *World War II, America at War, 1941-1945,* Random House, New York, 1991, 488

[3] *Ibid.*

4   Barger, Melvin D.: *Large Slow Target, Vol. II,* copyright 1989, United States LST Association, Taylor Publishing Co., Dallas, Tex., 15-16

5   *Dictionary of American Fighting Ships, Vol. VII,* James L. Mooney, editor, Naval Historical Center, Department of the Navy, Washington, D.C., 1981, 570

6   Barger *(op. cit.)* 21-23

7   *Ibid.*

8   Morison, Samuel Eliot: *History of U.S. Naval Operations in World War II, Vol. VII, Victory in the Pacific, 1945,* Little, Brown and Company, New York, 1976, 189

9   *Ibid.*

10   Alexander, Joseph H.: *Storm Landings; Epic Amphibious Battles in Central Pacific,* Naval Institute Press, Annapolis, 1997, 37

11   *Dictionary, op. cit.,* 571

12   *Ibid.*

13   *Ibid.,* 662

1

Parting Is Tough

*Fran and I end our "vacation" in New Orleans when
the LST 698 comes into port. Ralph Hart and I report aboard,
and Fran returns to Wilmette*

June 1944—"Ensign Ralph Hart and Ensign Homer Haswell:
LST 698 is here. You will report aboard immediately." That is the word
we received on 2 June 1944 at the New Orleans Naval Base. (Ralph
was my alphabetically related friend from midshipman school whom
I had met a few days earlier.)

My wife Fran and I had been enjoying nearly three weeks of
"honeymooning" in New Orleans, waiting for the *LST 698* to come
down the river from Jeffersonville, Ind. Now that the ship had arrived,
we knew our remaining hours and minutes together would pass all
too swiftly.

(We had met in May 1942, when Frances Marie Ellis was living at
home in Wilmette, Ill., and I was a yeoman in the Navy's District
Security office at Great Lakes. We were married that October. In 1944
I enrolled in midshipman school, Abbott Hall, Chicago, and on
graduation Ralph Hart, of St. Louis, and I were assigned to *LST 698*.)

Each day Ralph and I had reported at the Navy Base in Algiers,
across the river from New Orleans. The rest of the day Fran and I

wandered through the Vieux Carré, played tennis in Audubon Park and City Park, swam in Lake Pontchartrain, took trolley cars here and there, tried out one restaurant after another.

Then on 2 June, when Ralph's name and mine were called out at the afternoon muster, we collected all our per diem money, had our orders endorsed, and watched a typical New Orleans downpour (all over in 20 minutes). When the rain stopped, we caught a boat ride to the ship, which was tied up at the dock.

The quarterdeck was a big puddle, and the men were working with brooms. Bill Eklund, a young blond fellow from Austin, Texas, (known as Ek to fellow officers) was officer of the deck (O.D.). He introduced us to a somewhat older and heavier officer, Ken Saunders (Sandy), of Oakmont, Pa., the executive officer, and to Captain Glen Gilbert, of Grayson, La.

Captain Gilbert was a seasoned veteran—tall, black-haired, swarthy—a "mustang" who had been a chief quartermaster in the regular Navy. He had gone to officers' school and then became a lieutenant when he was given command of our ship.

The captain welcomed us aboard and told Ralph he would be assistant first lieutenant, reporting to Bill Eklund, in connection with general upkeep of the ship. I was to be assistant navigator, reporting to Sandy. After a brief chat, Ralph and I returned to New Orleans in one of the ship's boats.

I didn't return to the hotel until about six. Fran knew why I was delayed. We dressed for dinner, which in this case meant Fran's long dress and my dress whites. Fran helped me with the three hooks and eyes in the collar, over the Adam's apple.

We had dinner at the St. Charles. Then we quietly packed our luggage, being careful for once to put my razor in *my* suitcase and her bobby pins in *hers*. We divided up our cash (we had some, at last) and went to bed early. We didn't get much sleep. All we could think of was that this was the last night for *so* long—perhaps a year, perhaps two. Who could predict?

After breakfast, we put our suitcases on the elevator. Then, after loading my suitcase and seabag into the cab, I kissed Fran once more. It was tough. Fran promised not to cry, and she didn't. But I felt choked up as I bumped over the New Orleans streets in the cab, down to the boat landing.

As soon as I left, Fran took a cab to the airport and returned to Wilmette. Later I read over and over the sweet note she gave me when we parted—things both of us felt but neither of us could say at that time.

Over the next year everything that we had said and done together seemed to come back nearly as vividly as that day. And I knew from these things that she loved me, and I knew that she knew I loved her.

I just hoped it would not be too long before we could be together again at last. I lived for that day.

2

Fitting Her Out and
Shaking Her Down

Our LST is commissioned. We receive alterations,
supplies and provisions. Then at Panama City, Fla., we
practice beaching and drills and in Gulfport, Miss., we
load the tank deck with Quonset huts. Back in New Orleans,
they hoist a Landing Craft Tank (LCT) onto our main
deck. We're ready to go

June 1944—Ralph Hart and I arrived at the ship at 0800 on 3
June 1944, and shortly were invited to the tank deck for the ship's
commissioning. In that little ceremony *LST 698* became an official
navy ship and Lt. Glen W. Gilbert of Grayson, La., assumed command.

The rest of the officers and the crew had drilled in amphibious
training for two months at Camp Bradford, Md., on Chesapeake Bay.
They boarded the ship in Jeffersonville, Ind., at the Jeffersonville
Boat and Machine Company, and began to familiarize themselves
with their new assignments as they sailed down the Ohio and
Mississippi to New Orleans.

Ralph and I were assigned a room about 8 by 10 feet, with a
double-deck bunk along the outside bulkhead. Ralph took the

upper bunk. The room had a desk, a medicine cabinet with mirror, and a long clothes rack. No washbowl—we shaved in the head (washroom).

We met the other officers: Ed Erickson (Eric), a quiet, blond senior officer from Moorhead, Minn., supply officer; Bill Chapman, a personable fellow with a Southern accent, from Greenville, S.C., communication officer; Angelo Prezioso (known as "the chief"), a whimsical engineering officer from Youngstown, Ohio; and a gunnery officer named Ray Kennedy, from Oakville, Conn.

After we were given a tour of the ship, we were quickly put to work. That first day, Ralph served on the 1600 to 2000 watch and I followed him from 2000 hours to midnight.

One day (and through the night) we took on provisions at the Naval Supply Depot. Another day we loaded ammunition at the Naval Ammunition Depot. Welders and shipfitters came aboard to fit the ship with additional items like the mast and radar antenna. They also made design changes that could not be built in during original construction.

For example, it was necessary to raise the conning tower (conn) about eight feet, because we had six LCVP (landing craft vehicle, personnel) boats, with six sets of boat davits (two forward, four aft) instead of the usual two. The higher elevation gave us better visibility with those two big boats up forward. The extra space beneath the conn was made into a sea cabin for the skipper, where he could be reached at a moment's notice.

All this required a little more time in port. From our recreation fund we were able to pick up some softballs and basketballs and also some phonograph records.

In a few days we started on our shakedown cruise to Panama City, Fla. I watched carefully as the crew cast off the lines and we got underway. A pilot came aboard and they hauled down the "George" flag (we need a pilot) and ran up "How" (have pilot aboard).

This pilot easily qualified as a most colorful character in the Mark Twain tradition. He was a raconteur of the old school, and the hundred miles to the Gulf were filled nonstop with his stories. He seemed to prefer to face the stern rather than the bow and would interrupt his narrative when he recognized a landmark. He'd give the helmsman "right five" or "left five," followed by "midships." When we reached the pilot station at the South Channel and he disembarked, the ship seemed suddenly quiet.

Most of the river from New Orleans to the South Channel was about the same width as at New Orleans. But about 20 miles from the mouth it split into three separate channels (or more). Two of these were navigable by ships. But you'd never guess it was the Mississippi. Our channel narrowed to perhaps 150 feet in width. On each side was a desolate-looking swamp—a center of Louisiana's fur-trapping industry.

At St. Andrew's Bay (Panama City, Fla.), we found numerous other LSTs. Together we went through a complete regimen of drills—general quarters, fire, fire and rescue, abandon ship, man overboard—until we became familiar with our tasks and sufficiently proficient.

For several days we practiced beaching—running the ship full speed into the shore until it came to rest on the sand. Beaching had always been the unforgivable sin for which a skipper could be court-martialed, For us greenhorns it became a standard procedure. On islands which had no docks, beaching became a highly efficient means for loading or unloading troops, vehicles and supplies—our primary responsibility in the war.

Lou Miller of Burlingame, Calif., and Bruce Montgomery of St. Paul, Minn., both teachers, reported for duty as boat officers on 14 June, together with 16 men (four boat crews). This enabled us to operate all six boats at one time whenever necessary. Three days later we had a beaching drill in which all six boats were put into the water at once for beaching practice.

We had tactical maneuvers with ten other LSTs on 18 June and on the next day had towing and fueling exercises and night maneuvers. The same exercises we had done in the daytime were much trickier at night.

We worked with *LST 671,* towing that ship to the beach and then pulling it off. Another day we practiced docking exercises and further drills, including collision drills and night beaching, mooring to another LST, together with more general quarters, man overboard, and fire and rescue drills.

An inspection of ship and personnel on our final day at Panama City included a battle problem and more general drills. Each ship was graded for competency, and we learned we received very high marks.

We sailed to Gulfport, Miss., where we loaded our first cargo into the tank deck through the huge bow doors. The bow ramp, which in its vertical position provided a seal for the bow when the ship was underway, was lowered forward on beaching until it reached the ground, permitting vehicles to move directly into the tank deck.

A second ramp could be lowered to provide access to the main deck. Although these ships were originally conceived for hauling tanks and amphibious craft, we quickly found they hauled everything imaginable.

The first cargo for our LST turned out to be Quonset huts. The whole tank deck was soon filled solid with the prefabricated parts for these buildings, used as basic structures in the forward bases of the Pacific. We were amazed to watch how fast the fork-lift operator could speed into the ship with a load, discharge it, and whirl around to pick up another.

A day or two later we returned to New Orleans for final fix-ups. In the morning I got up and went to the head in my shorts—and ran into four lady welders! Workers were swarming aboard to give our LST a standard set of revisions. They tore stuff out from one area and welded it down somewhere else. Painters splashed paint here and a different color there.

We took the ship through the degaussing range to neutralize the magnetic field of the ship. One of the men teased a younger seaman, telling him he'd have to be degaussed. *"Nobody's* going to get me degaussed," the seaman said emphatically.

At another dock a giant crane set an entire LCT (landing *craft tank* used in harbor work) on our main deck—an expeditious way to get these craft to a "forward area." It was to sit there occupying a major part of the deck for the next four months. The LCT's skipper and crew came aboard as passengers.

At last, more than a month after the ship was commissioned, we were ready. We received our orders to get underway: ComEight Secret Dispatch 061734. Destination: Cristobal, Canal Zone.

3

It Wasn't *JUST* Pearl Harbor; How Japanese Attacks Brought U.S. into the War

The attack on Pearl Harbor was matched the same day by simultaneous blows on Malaya, Hong Kong, and the Philippines. Thousands killed. Many ships and planes destroyed. AND the American people became aroused

Now that we knew we were headed for the Panama Canal and the Pacific Ocean, let's recall what got us into this war in the first place.

Early in December 1941, we knew that we would soon be at war—with Germany. The war in Europe had been going on since 1939, and our eyes as a nation had been focused on Europe. We had been complacent about the actions of the Japanese.

For four years the Japanese had been at war with China. They had occupied Formosa, now known as Taiwan, as well as many coastal cities on the mainland and major parts of Manchuria. In the Pacific the islands of the Carolines, Marshalls, and Marianas (except Guam) were part of a 1920 Japanese mandate. The Japanese had built up their fleet and armed forces immensely. But their oil was in short supply, and they had their eyes on the oil fields in the East Indies and Malaya.

Suddenly on 7 December 1941 our nation received a jolt:
JAPANESE ATTACK PEARL HARBOR!

Nearly all of us who were alive on that Sunday afternoon can remember where we were when we heard the news. But in Tokyo these were the headlines:

WAR IS ON
JAPAN's NAVY PLANES ATTACK HAWAII
SINGAPORE, DAVAO, WAKE, GUAM

JAPANESE TROOP TRANSPORT OFF HAWAII.
GREAT SUCCESSES REPORTED IN ALL AREAS
RAIDED IN NAVAL ANNOUNCEMENT.
BRITISH TROOPS IN THAILAND BEING WIPED
OUT.
HONGKONG HEAVILY BOMBED BY NAVY.
—LANDING IN MALAYA ANNOUNCED.
—CABINET MEETING IN EMERGENCY
SESSION.[1]

The Japanese planes that swooped down on Pearl Harbor that Sunday morning caught our forces by surprise. Instantly the lives of Americans everywhere were drastically changed.

This was not a raid. It was a full-scale striking force including "six of the newest and largest carriers of the Imperial Navy, a screen of nine destroyers and a light cruiser, a support force of two battleships and two heavy cruisers; three fleet submarines to patrol the flanks, and a supply train of seven or eight tankers."[2]

They had traveled a far northerly route from Japan to avoid detection and then approached Hawaii from the north instead of from the west. Separately, 27 submarines had proceeded on a more direct route, refueling at Kwajalein. When the fleet reached a point 275 miles north of Pearl Harbor, 183 planes were launched.

At 0750 they struck—the torpedo planes and dive bombers for "Battleship Row," the high-level bombers for Hickam Field, the fighters for Wheeler Field and the Kaneohe Naval Air Station. A second wave of 140 planes made their final approach from the east about 0900, with dive bombers concentrating on the ships in the harbor, while the horizontal bombers attacked the air fields. Zero fighters strafed and provided top cover. This time, although the defenses were better and the Japanese met a hail of gunfire, they still inflicted considerable damage. At 1000 hours it was all over and the planes formed up to return to their carriers.

Harry A. Gailey summed it up in *War in the Pacific, from Pearl Harbor to Tokyo Bay:*

> Yamamoto's plan had succeeded beyond the wildest dreams of the Japanese high command in Tokyo. The task force had lost only 29 planes, one large submarine, and five midget submarines. Only 55 fliers had been killed. On the opposite side of the ledger, his airmen had sunk the battleships *Arizona, Oklahoma* and *Utah,* as well as the destroyers *Downes* and *Cassin.* This was not the full story, however. The battleships *West Virginia, Nevada* and *California* and the minelayer *Oglala* were sunk but later raised and repaired. The battleships *Tennessee, Pennsylvania* and *Maryland,* the cruisers *Honolulu, Helena,* and *Raleigh,* the destroyer *Shaw,* and the service ships *Vestal* and *Curtiss* were all damaged. The navy lost 92 planes and had an additional 31 damaged. A total of 2,008 navy personnel were killed and 710 wounded. The Marine Corps had 109 killed and 69 wounded. There were 103 civilian casualties including 68 dead. The army also suffered heavily . . . In all, 96 Army aircraft were destroyed and 128 damaged. Army casualties numbered 218 killed and 364 wounded. Hangars and storage facilities at all the airfields were either destroyed or badly damaged . . . . [3]

The next day, 8 December, President Roosevelt addressed Congress to ask for a formal declaration of war. His first words were long remembered by those who heard him on the radio: "Yesterday, December 7, 1941—a date which will live in infamy—the United

States was suddenly and deliberately attacked . . ." Congress declared war within an hour. Three days later, Hitler declared war against the United States. Historian Gailey remarked: "All pretense of neutrality regarding the war in Europe was gone. America would fight the two-front war that the U. S. planners envisioned in their worst-case scenario. Japan's success at Pearl Harbor had united America as never before."[4]

The Japanese lost no time in following up on the Pearl Harbor attack. In fact, half an hour *before* that attack (but on December 8 on the western side of the International Date Line) they had made landings on the Philippines, Siam and northern Malaya. Hong Kong was attacked on that same day, as were Guam and Wake. The attack on Pearl Harbor was part of the Japanese plan, which involved simultaneous advances toward the Philippines, Dutch East Indies, and Malaya. Henry Michel wrote, in *The Second World War:*

> The operation was to be carried out in two phases. In the first phase, Hong Kong, Wake and Guam would be occupied and troops landed in the Philippines and Malaya; in the second phase the Dutch East Indies, Singapore and Burma would be conquered. In the east, no advance would be made beyond a line joining the Kurile, Wake and Gilbert Islands, the north coast of New Guinea, Timor, and the northern Solomon Islands. In the southwest the main stronghold would be Rabaul.
>
> In these plans the attack on Pearl Harbor was in fact considered as an hors d'oeuvre, a preliminary tactical operation on a grand scale reserved for the Navy, the success of which would make it easier to carry out the rest of the scheme. And indeed for the first few months, everything took place as planned.[5]

One by one they fell. Guam on 10 December, 1941; Wake on 23 December; Hong Kong, 25 December; Singapore and Rabaul in January; Malaya in February; Dutch East Indies in March; Philippines in April; major parts of New Guinea, 9 February to 19 April; Guadalcanal in May.

In less than half a year the Japanese captured islands and mainland strongholds in vast reaches of the southwest Pacific. They were well on their way in assembling their "Greater East Asia Co-Prosperity Sphere,"[6] with operations spreading "across the International Date Line and seven time zones."[7]

Notes

[1]   Hoyt, Edwin P.: *Japan's War: The Great Pacific Conflict, 1853 to 1952*, McGraw-Hill Book Company, New York, 228-9

[2]   Morison, Samuel Eliot: *The Two-Ocean War*, Little, Brown and Company, New York, 1963, 39

[3]   Gailey, Harry A.: *War in the Pacific, from Pearl Harbor to Tokyo Bay*, Presidio Press, Novato, CA, 1995, 96. Permission obtained from Random House, Inc.

[4]   *Ibid.*, 99

[5]   Michel, Henri: *The Second World War*, Praeger Publishers, New York, Washington, 1975, 335. Permission obtained from Greenwood Publishing Group, Inc.

[6]   *American Heritage Pictorial Atlas of United States History*, American Heritage Publishing Co., New York, 292

[7]   *The Times Atlas of the Second World War*, John Keegan, editor, Harper & Row, Publishers, New York, 1989, 68

4

First Western Pacific Allied Footholds

Japanese solidify Pacific empire, ranging from Aleutians to Dutch East Indies. First American victory comes in May 1942 in Coral Sea, quickly followed by Battle of Midway. Island hopping invasions begin

The Japanese juggernaut continued to solidify its control over the vast empire it had been building, island by island:

- Rabaul, in New Britain, and Singapore, both of which became major staging bases
- Brunei, Sarawak, Borneo, Sumatra, Java, Timor
- Finschafen and Lae in Northeast New Guinea; Hollandia in Dutch New Guinea
- Bougainville and Tulagi in the Solomons
- Even the U. S. islands of Attu and Kiska in the Aleutians.

The first American victory came on 8 May 1942 in the battle of Coral Sea. It was the first carrier engagement in history. Though the *Lexington* was sunk, the Japanese had to call off their invasion of Port

Moresby, Papua New Guinea, and withdrew. According to the *Times Atlas of the Second World War,* "It proved to be the point at which the flow of Japanese successes in the area was finally stemmed, allowing the Allies to gradually consolidate their strengths."[1]

Then came the battle of Midway, 4 to 6 June 1942. Admiral Yamamoto had planned his attack to take Midway Island and, if possible, locate and destroy any American fleet that attempted to intercept him. Yamamoto had sent two of his carriers and a large force to Dutch Harbor, Alaska, as a diversion, to draw our forces away from the main event. But thanks to the breaking of the Japanese code, our forces at Pearl Harbor had learned of the plan. "The losses for the Japanese at Midway were horrendous," according to Historian D. Clayton James. "Four carriers, 275 planes and 3,500 men killed. In contrast the Americans lost one carrier [the *Yorktown*], 132 planes and 307 men dead."[2]

This battle ended the threat to Midway and to Pearl Harbor. As another historian, Harry A. Gailey, assessed it:

> With such security, Nimitz could begin to assemble what would ultimately be the overpowering Fifth Fleet. He could later pick his objectives without fear of Japanese attack. Hawaii thus became the main supply base for the Pacific war. The Japanese commanders in turn became defensive, not willing to risk the main elements of the Combined Fleet in another major engagement. This led them to abandon plans for the conquest of Fiji, New Caledonia, and New Zealand. There would be other critical naval engagements before the end of the war, but none with the disastrous potential that a victory by Yamamoto's grand fleet would have posed . . . [3]

The Japanese moved into the Solomons in the summer of 1942—first Tulagi on 3 May, then Guadalcanal, where they started immediately to construct an airfield. On 7 August our forces landed 19,000 Marines in our "first amphibian operation . . . since 1898 [in Cuba]."[4] Historian Morison told us, in the introduction to his 40-page chapter on "Guadalcanal" in *Two-Ocean War:*

> The Guadalcanal campaign, the most bitterly contested
> in American history since the Campaign of Northern Virginia
> in the Civil War, comprised seven major naval engagements,
> at least ten pitched land battles, and innumerable forays,
> bombardments and skirmishes.[5]

By February 1943 the Japanese had evacuated 10,652 troops. They had lost Guadalcanal at the cost of 20,000 troops, 860 aircraft, and 15 warships.[6] And with it, an end to Japanese expansion in the Pacific.

Ships, planes, troops, and supplies were being rushed from the United States to all the war areas in the western and southwestern Pacific. In 1943 alone American shipyards "put into service a warship tonnage equivalent to that of the total Imperial Navy at the outbreak of the war."[7] New carriers, new battleships, new destroyers, and new amphibious vessels were produced in great numbers.

In the earliest amphibious operations personnel and cargo were transferred from transports into amphtracs (LVTs) and landing boats (LCVPs). But when the LSTs arrived in the forward areas, they were promptly accepted for their ability to carry their loads right up to the beach without transferring them to the boats—a vast saving in time and often an avoidance of danger. Admiral Daniel B. Barbey noted, referring to the southwest Pacific operations:

> This moving of whole communities of 30,000 men and
> their equipment—in the case of the Hollandia operation,
> more than 100,000—was made possible because of the slow,
> awkward, wonderful LSTs; the ships whose construction was
> turned down just three years previously, in the belief that
> they would fulfill no need in a modern war. When war did
> come a few weeks later, a more realistic appraisal was made
> and construction was started on more than 1,000 of these
> LSTs. Without them it is difficult to imagine how the war
> could have been successfully fought.[8]

For these operations the Fifth Amphibious Force was set up within the Fifth Fleet to operate in the Central Pacific under Admiral Nimitz, while the Seventh Amphibious Force operated in the Southwest Pacific, under General MacArthur and the Seventh Fleet. These two groups nipped away at enemy positions through 1943 and 1944.

In the meantime the Fast Carrier Forces of the Fifth and Seventh Fleets had hit Truk, in the Carolines, and Rabaul, in New Britain, so hard and so often that these two Japanese strongholds were rendered neutralized and hence were not invaded. In a single day, 17 February 1944, "Mitscher's carrier planes raided Truk, destroying 200,000 tons of shipping and 275 aircraft, with few American losses."[9] Rabaul had been similarly neutralized in November 1943 and was henceforth bypassed.

Vast portions of the Pacific thus became, in a sense, an American sea, where American ships could sail with relative safety. At the same time the arrival of more and more American ships, planes and troops gave the Americans a sense of confidence that was rare a year before.

*　　*　　*

We were aware of very little of this when we in our LST 698 were sailing through the Caribbean to join those veterans who had made the trip a year or two years earlier and had participated in those early invasions. But when we visited Guadalcanal and the bases shown in italics in the table that follows, we were mindful of the blood and sweat that went into seizing those lands from the Japanese.

Main Operations of 5th and 7th Amphibious Forces

In the Central Pacific[10]   In the Southwest Pacific[11]
(*Italics* indicate bases visited by LST 698)

Gilberts—Makin and Tarawa	21 Nov 1943	Woodlark and Kiriwina	30 Jun 1943
Marshalls—Majura	31 Jan 1944	New Guinea, Lae	16 Sep 1943
Marshalls, Kwajalein	31 Jan to 4 Feb 1944	*New Guinea, Finschhafen*	22 Sep 1943
Eniwetok	17 to 23 Feb 1944	New Britain, Arawe	15 Dec 1943
Marianas, Saipan	15 Jun-24 Jul 1944	New Britain, Cape Gloucester	26 Dec 1943
Marianas, Guam	21 Jul 1944	New Guinea, Saidor	2 Jan 1944
Palau	15 Sep 1944	*Admiralties, Manus and Los Negros*	Mar 1944
Carolines, Ulithi	23 Sep 1944	*Dutch New Guinea, Hollandia*	22 Apr 1944
Ngulu	16 Oct 1944	Dutch New Guinea, Wakde	17 May 1944
Iwo Jima	19 Feb 1945	*Schouten Islands, Biak*	27 May 1944
		Noemfoor	2 Jul 1944
		Sansapor	30 Jul 1944
		Netherlands East Indies, Morotai	15 Sep 1944

Notes

1. *Times Atlas of the Second World War,* John Keenan, editor, Harper & Row Publishers New York, 1989, 75

2. James, D. Clayton, and Anne Sharp Wells: *From Pearl Harbor to V-J Day, The American Armed Forces in World War II,* American Way Series, Ivan R. Dee, Chicago, 121

3. Gailey, Harry A.: *The War in the Pacific, from Pearl Harbor to Tokyo Bay,* Presidio Press, Novato, CA, 1995, 170. Permission granted by Random House, Inc.

4. Morison, Samuel Eliot: *The Two-Ocean War,* Little, Brown and Company, New York, 1963, 141

5. *Ibid.,* 139 *et seq.* (This 40-page chapter tells the story in great detail. Guadalcanal is also the main topic of *Volume V* of Morison's *History of United States Naval Operations in World War II, The Struggle for Guadalcanal, August 1942- February 1943,* Little, Brown and Company, New York, 1959.)

6. *Times Atlas, op. cit.,* 121

7. *Ibid.,* 122

8. Barbey, Daniel E.: *MacArthur's Amphibious Navy,* Naval Institute Press Annapolis, 1969, 216

9. James, *op. cit.,* 138

10. Alexander, Joseph H.: *Storm Landings, Epic Amphibious Battles in the Central Pacific,* Naval Institute Press, Annapolis, 1997 (describes the Central Pacific invasions)

11. Barbey, *op. cit.* (an excellent source for the Southwest Pacific landings)

5

The Blue Caribbean Beckons, Threatens

We discuss the self-sufficiency of the crew, day-to-day operations, watch duties, "shooting" the stars. Guantanamo Bay. As we head for the Panama Canal, our first big storm throws a file cabinet around

July 1944—Our departure from New Orleans seemed like an anticlimax after the furious days spent in getting everything aboard. We now had the big LCT (landing craft tank) on our main deck ahead of the bridge. Our tank deck was loaded to the gills with prefabricated Quonset huts. The magazines were filled with ammunition, and our food lockers and freezers were crammed with provisions of all kinds, including about six-months' supply of meats in the freezer. The charthouse had a large inventory of charts, focused on portfolios for the Pacific areas.

Our fuel tanks were filled with diesel fuel, and our water tanks contained an abundance of fresh water. We had an inventory of spare parts, some for periodic replacement, while others were major parts such as a propeller screw and an extra shaft, which were part of a pool for ships in our group.

We were self-sufficient in other ways. Our officers and men, with the exception of Ralph Hart and me who had come directly from midshipman school, had spent two months or more in an amphibious school in Maryland, learning their duties as a crew. And while regular Navy officers were given broad training to let them take over any position to which they were assigned, the reserve officers were given the rudiments of seamanship, navigation and gunnery, plus a single specialization, and sent to war.

Each ship had to be able to function independently. The deck hands could handle the lines, the helmsman steered the ship, the baker baked the bread. There had also been training in numerous specialties. For example, Charles Sofield, an electrician from Perth Amboy, N.J., was given special instruction in refrigeration, while Richard Alexander, of Calvert City, Ky., had learned all about the gyrocompass.

Most of our officers and men were young. Our skipper, Captain Gilbert, was just 26 but had spent seven years in the regular navy. Because of recognition of his ability, he had graduated from chief quartermaster into officer ranks. Bill Eklund, "first lieutenant" in charge of all the deck hands, was too young to vote in the 1944 election. Fewer than a dozen of us had ever gone to sea before.

So here we were, cruising in the Gulf of Mexico on our way to who knows where.

A bit about day-to-day ship operation: When we were about to get under way or come in to port, we set the "special sea detail." Deck hands were stationed to handle the bow or stern anchor or mooring lines, with the first lieutenant in charge; the engineering officer was in the engine room, and other officers and men were in pre-assigned positions.

The captain and navigator were in the conn, along with the watch officers. (Although I was *assistant* navigator, I was stationed on the conn and Sandy, the executive officer and navigator, was in the forward gun tub.) The captain gave all orders, which were then relayed through the speaking tube to the helmsman and by telephone to the engine room and other locations. The communication officer and signalmen kept him apprised of all messages received by flag or blinker light, and the radioman immediately passed on radio messages. We had gyrocompass repeaters on both the conn (for the skipper and watch officers) and the bridge (for the helmsman).

Once the ship was outside the harbor and in its position in the convoy, the special sea detail was secured and the watch officers took over. Various petty officers and seamen were on watch in the conn, down in the engine room, the bow, and other locations. One watch officer "conned" the ship, directing its speed and direction.

Whenever anything unusual was taking place—special turns or unusually bad weather, for example—the captain took over. According to *Naval Regulations* ("Rocks and Shoals"), he was responsible at all times and must be informed of any change in course or speed, weather, lights sighted, other ships, and even the color of the water.

From the start we felt great confidence in our skipper. Though this was his first command, his seven years in the regular navy made him a seasoned veteran compared with the rest of us. He could see a ship come over the horizon faster than anyone else on the conn. He was the first to note when we gained on the ship ahead in the convoy. When he came to the conn and took over in some kind of crisis, we knew we were in good hands.

The ship traveled completely blacked out. Passageways, heads and the chart house were lighted with red "battle lights" all night. (Instead of red ink, all navigational charts used magenta, which could be seen under red light.) Normally, white lights could be used indoors, but for half an hour before going on watch, it was necessary to wear red goggles to adjust the eyes to darkness before going to the conn or to other outdoor locations.

Often it was extremely dark and practically impossible to see other ships in the convoy. We watched continuously through binoculars and kept a careful search. We traveled in a regular formation, so that each ship had a definite place. However, the ship ahead of us had a marvelous facility for being everywhere except that place.

Every day we had general quarters (manning the battle stations) for about an hour before sunrise and after sunset. Each man hurried to his assigned battle station. This is supposed to take place instantly when the alarm is sounded. One night I had come off watch at 0400, and the GQ alarm went off about 0530. I jumped out of bed in a complete daze but managed to start up the ladder to the bridge, tucking in my shirt with one hand, buttoning my pants with the other.

On these morning and evening GQs Sandy (the exec) and I got the sextant and prepared to "shoot the stars." In the evening we stood and waited for the first star to appear. We had a list of the positions of the six or seven brightest stars that would be visible that evening. One by one we shot them before the horizon faded. In the morning we located the selected stars and then waited for enough light to have a clear horizon, then hustled to get readings before the stars disappeared. We took the readings to the chart room to translate them into a new position on the chart (called a "fix").

On the morning of 14 July the Atlantic was a beautiful blue. For some time we saw Cuba to starboard. We cruised within sight of the eastern tip, rounded it, and turned west a few miles to Guantanamo Bay (only about 50 miles east of Santiago, where in 1898 the Spanish fleet had been bottled up and eventually destroyed).

We entered the bay and were directed to an anchorage. We had barely dropped anchor when we heard a plop. We saw concentric circles of muddy water. We had anchored in water barely 15 feet deep—just enough depth for our LST.

There wasn't much to see other than a few U. S. ships and an Officers' Club, where the officers went ashore to dine. In the Ship's Service store I bought a leather handbag for Fran—for about 12 bucks.

From Guantanamo we headed south toward the Panama Canal. It looked easy—sailing in the beautiful blue Caribbean. We stood our watches as the ship cruised smoothly along under a clear blue sky.

But the sea turned gray and got choppier and choppier. We thought we were prepared for this. For example, the tables in the wardroom and mess hall were welded to the deck and had removable edge boards. Just turn them over end for end, and they had a lip designed to save dishes from sliding off the table. But these didn't have much effect in a storm like this.

Things began to be thrown around. If I tried to walk, I found myself walking uphill one moment and downhill the next. Ed

Erickson, supply officer, had a big file cabinet in his stateroom. It had not yet been welded to the deck, and it began to slide all over the place. Suddenly it whipped up against the bulkhead, bending the steel outward into the passageway. The bulkhead remained bent for the rest of our cruise, reminding us of what the sea can do.

George Hickman, our steward's mate from Marion Station, Md., opened the wardroom refrigerator door and found nearly every dish broken and the contents spread all over the shelves.

Entering the Canal Zone, we pulled into Coco Solo Naval Base. We had a security briefing to emphasize the necessity for all officers and men to pay particular attention to their own safety if they left the base. Under no circumstance should anyone travel alone.

With that warning we took a bus into Cristobal. Lou Miller was my "buddy," and we had a splendid meal at a hotel owned by the Chase National Bank. We couldn't get over the quantity of butter served, considering its scarcity back home.

After dinner we wandered through the town. All the shops were open—bars, tattoo joints, etc. I was lured into buying some "genuine" nylon stockings which I sent home to Fran. Nylons had come on the market shortly before the war began, and the women found that they lasted far longer than silk—as long as six months. Since nylons were rationed back home, they were a hot item. Later I learned that these from Panama lasted only a week at most!

Everybody got back to the ship early. We were looking forward to going through the canal the next day.

6

Panama Canal, Shortcut to Pacific

*From Limon Bay we enter a series of concrete chasms
known as the Gatun Locks. We are lifted to Gatun Lake,
85 feet above the two oceans, then are lowered through locks
into the Pacific. Porpoises and flying fish accompany us to
our maneuvers in the Gulf of California*

July 1944—We were about to see first-hand one of the greatest
marvels of our age, the Panama Canal. David McCullough, in *The Path
Between the Seas,* dramatizes its historic impact:

> The creation of a water passage across Panama was one of
> the supreme human achievements of all time, the culmination
> of a heroic dream of 400 years and of more than 20 years of
> phenomenal effort and sacrifice. The 50 miles between the
> oceans were among the hardest ever won by human effort
> and ingenuity, and no statistics on tonnage or tolls can begin
> to convey the grandeur of what was accomplished. Primarily
> the canal is an expression of that old and noble desire to
> bridge the divide, to bring people together. It is a work of
> civilization.[1]

Most important was the reason it was built in the first place—to vastly shorten the time for ships that sailed from one ocean to the other. Looking at my own family history, what a difference the Panama Canal would have made to my great, great grandfather and grandmother!

Samuel and Nancy Ruggles had sailed from Boston Harbor in October, 1819, in the brig *Thaddeus* as members of the first company of American missionaries to Hawaii. It took them more than three months to reach a treacherous Cape Horn and two more months (late March) before they sighted the shores of Hawaii—a perilous voyage of five months. Sixteen years later they had reversed the route, returning to Connecticut.

The route through Panama would have shortened the distance from roughly 14,600 miles to 6,600 miles, saving 8,000 miles!

In the early 1860s my Grandfather Haswell had a somewhat easier journey, returning from California. He sailed from San Francisco to the Isthmus of Panama, took the new Panama Railroad to the Atlantic side, and then transferred to a ship bound for Boston.

But even with the railroad this was a treacherous, uncertain journey through steamy jungles plagued with yellow fever, malaria, and other tropical diseases.

To me these reflections add a personal dimension to the thrill of cruising through the Panama Canal, one of the most formidable construction projects ever attempted, to be completed at a cost of unknown hundreds, perhaps thousands, of lives.

We got under way early that morning and cruised across Colon Harbor and Limon Bay to the entrance to the canal. A few ships were ahead of us as we awaited our turn to enter Gatun Locks.

A locomotive or "mule" towed us into the open lock chamber, 110 feet wide and 1,000 feet long, and we took our position with other naval ships. The sidewalls were high above us, and we seemed to be at the bottom of a canyon. The locks closed, and we watched the water flow in. Eventually the water rose to the level of the second lock. The gates opened ahead of us, and the mule towed us into the second lock.

We were again in a deep trench, with the lock's walls rising high above us. The gates behind us closed, the water poured in, and we rose with it. The process was repeated once more until, when the gates opened ahead of us, we moved out of the third lock into Gatun Lake, 85 feet above the Caribbean and Limon Bay. McCullough refers to the locks as "the structural triumphs at Panama."

> In their overall dimensions, mass, weight, in the mechanisms and ingenious control apparatus incorporated in their design, they surpassed any similar structures in the world. They were, as was often said, the mighty portals of the Panama Gateway. Yet they were something much more than monumental; they did not, like a bridge or a cathedral, just stand there; they *worked.* They were made of concrete and they were made of literally thousands of moving parts. Large essential elements were not built, but were manufactured, made in Pittsburgh, Wheeling, Schenectady, and other cities. In a very real sense they were colossal machines, the largest yet conceived, and in their final, finished form they would function quite as smoothly as a Swiss watch. They were truly one of the engineering triumphs of all time . . . . [2]

We found ourselves in the long and broad Gatun Lake, surrounded by hills and forests, and we traveled some 24 miles through the lake (about half the total length of the canal). Gatun Lake stretched out to cover all the lower areas. It is said to have a shoreline 1,100 miles long!

Eventually we left the lake and entered a pass with tall banks on both sides. This was the famous Culebra Cut, now known as the Gaillard Cut. This was the scene of the greatest amount of earth moving in the canal's construction, cutting a channel through the Continental Divide. In all, some 262 million cubic yards were excavated.[3]

To bring us down to sea level on the Pacific side, we entered the Pedro Miguel Locks, sailed out through the Miraflores Lake, and then through the two sets of Miraflores Locks.

Although the sea level is the same for the Atlantic and Pacific oceans, the Pacific has 20-foot tides, while the Atlantic tide is nominal at this point. The canal brought us to Balboa and to the southern tip of Panama City.

After we passed the breakwater, we turned west and headed up the coast toward San Diego. A school of porpoises began to escort us through the Pacific. Flying fish seemed to glide about two feet above the surface for some 15 feet and then drop back into the water.

One of the routines we settled into was also one of the least pleasant—the censorship of mail. When the quantity required it, three or four officers would sit around a table in the wardroom and go through the mail that had been written by the enlisted men.

It was embarrassing to have to go through the love letters to wives and sweethearts, and this censorship surely put a damper on what they wished to say. But the Navy had to guard against revealing to anyone where we had been and where we were going. The men knew that, too, but some were a little naive. I remember one man's writing something like this: "I can't tell you where we are, but sometimes they call this the 'big ditch.'" A few days later he wrote, "I can't tell you where we are, but it reminds me of the song, 'Down Mexico Way.'"

On August 3 I had a birthday cake. The captain and Sandy got the idea that it would be nice to make a list of all the birthdays of the ship's crew and have individual birthday cakes for them. When they found out that mine had just passed, they asked the cook to fix up a birthday cake for me anyhow—with inscription: "July 16—gone but not forgotten." It was quite a surprise!

When we reached the Gulf of California at the base of Mexico's Baja peninsula, we sailed into the gulf for about half a day of drills and maneuvers. We saw a couple of seals jumping completely out of the water, twisting and waving their flippers.

In a few days we were in San Diego Harbor. We took on more supplies and provisions. When leaving for a forward area, each ship was loaded with as much as it could carry.

I was able to call Fran and tell her where I was. She had just talked with Nan Orwig, whom we had double-dated with in 1942. It turned out that Nan's fiancé, Wade Drake, was stationed at the San Diego Naval Base. I arranged to see him, and by some connivance he gave me a birthday gift from Fran—Mendelssohn's *Italian Symphony*. In the months ahead, it was good to have that album along.

Notes

[1] McCullough, David: *The Path Between the Seas; the Creation of the Panama Canal, 1870-1914,* Simon & Schuster, New York, 1977, 613. These quotations are reprinted with permission of Simon & Schuster Adult Publishing Group from *The Path Between the Seas,* copyright 1977 by David McCullough

[2] *Ibid.,* 590

[3] *Ibid.,* 611

7

Guitars, Infantry, Drills off Maui

*As we headed for Hawaii and the tropics, we saw
thousands of stars, heard siren songs; we unloaded the
Quonset huts, took on troops and amphibious tanks of the
96th Infantry Division, damaged our bow ramp in exercises
off Maui*

August 1944—We pulled out of the harbor at San Diego, entered
the deep blue waters of the Pacific, and realized we were truly on our
way. We put away the charts for North and Central America and hauled
out the Hawaii portfolio.

(We had noted at the start, in New Orleans, that we had chart
portfolios for a good part of the Pacific and nothing for Europe,
confirming our expectations that we were headed for the Pacific
theater. And at Abbott Hall (midshipmen's school), we could dream
of a cruiser or a carrier, but nearly every graduate in our class was
assigned to the amphibious service.)

For the first 300 miles or so the Pacific was not so pacific as we
expected. It was fairly choppy. But then it became a beautiful blue,
with blue skies and gentle cumulus clouds. Cruising on a
southwesterly course, we began to feel that we were indeed heading
for the tropics.

And the nights—we saw stars by the thousands, more than we had ever seen in our lives. We began to recognize the brightest ones and watched them as they passed from east to west across the sky.

I began to work more intensively with Sandy (Ken Saunders, the executive officer) on morning and evening star sights. We went out on deck about 20 minutes before sunrise and started looking for the six or seven best navigational stars for that particular morning. And about 20 minutes before *sunset,* we'd watch for the first evening stars to appear.

Using the sextant, we measured the altitude of five or six stars— the angle the star made with the horizon—and marked the precise time. Then we returned to the charthouse to make our calculations. First we entered the Nautical Almanac, which contained the altitudes of the 60 navigational stars and the visible planets, based on "assumed positions" at specific latitudes. We then made calculations to compare these altitudes with the ones we had just obtained with the sextant.

At one time navigators had used a complicated procedure involving spherical trigonometry. But during the depression, the WPA (Works Progress Administration) developed a set of tables, comprising eight volumes, for the U. S. Hydrographic Office. These were published as *H. O. 214,* and the Navy was ever grateful, because it reduced the calculations to a few additions and subtractions.

The result was a position line on the navigation chart for each star, at right angles to the star's azimuth (direction), at a calculated distance from the assumed position. If the readings and calculations were correct, the perpendicular position lines for three or more stars would intersect, and that would be our new position (or *fix).*

This is an oversimplification, we know, but all of this is obsolete, anyhow. Celestial navigation was first replaced by loran, based on one's position in relation to signals from two loran stations. And now a computer can give an automatic readout of your position, based on navigational satellites.

Celestial navigation is just one of the forms of navigation we used. Within sight of land we had *piloting,* based on visual sighting of landmarks or, where there were any, such aids to navigation as lights and buoys. In addition we had *radar.*

Sailing westward, when we passed from one time zone to the next, the unlucky guys on watch got an extra hour of watch.

Our crossing to Hawaii was uneventful until we came within 200 miles. Then the ship's radio pulled in some strumming guitars and ukuleles. They were like a siren song, happy and carefree, luring us toward the islands.

We sailed past Diamond Head, Waikiki, and downtown Honolulu. Planes were landing and taking off from Hickam Field and Ford Island. We entered Pearl Harbor and were directed into the West Loch.

One of our crew had the thrill of a lifetime. His brother had been out in the Pacific two years. You can imagine his excitement when he not only saw his brother's ship but realized that our ship was assigned to moor alongside it.

This was no shiny LST like ours. It had battle scars and plenty of rust. Bullet holes on the bridge and three small Bettys painted on the conn. It had just returned from the invasion of Saipan, and the crew was full of sea stories.

Once in port, everyone scurried around the base for more supplies. In doing such errands we were lucky, because of our having six LCVP landing craft instead of two. We had many opportunities to view the harbor. One of the first sights was what was left of the *West Virginia*.

Sandy had big news in the mail—a baby daughter! (I hadn't told anyone about our own news in prospect and did not intend to right away.)

Everyone had liberty at least once. Most of the men got as far as the sailor traps in downtown Honolulu, but I went with some of the officers to Waikiki. The chief attractions at that time were the Moana Hotel and the famed Royal Hawaiian, where rows of tall royal palms then lined the long sidewalk from Kalakaua Boulevard to the front entrance. Between the two hotels was the Outrigger Club, with numerous catamarans and outrigger canoes. We went for a swim.

After unloading our Quonset huts, we eventually took on 17 officers and 269 enlisted men of the 96th Army Infantry Division, plus their amphibious tanks. About half of the men were assigned bunks, while the rest prepared to sleep on the main deck or in vehicles.

We sailed with a large group of LSTs of Task Force 33.6 for exercises in Maalaea Bay off Maui, near the sugar islands of Kahoolawe and Lanai, to give the troops experience in disembarking their amphibious tanks (LVTs) through the bow doors into the sea and churning through the water to the beach.

In the course of the exercise, the port and starboard sides of our bow ramp were sheared from their foundations, and the cables, both port and starboard, parted. We retired to the lee side of Kahoolawe Island to rig an emergency hoist on the bow ramp.

The tank deck filled with three feet of water.[1] Ballast pumps and an emergency fire pump emptied a ballast tank and cleared the water from the tank deck. The bow ramp was finally closed, and we sailed for Blue Beach, Keawakapu, Maui, "with 14 LVTs and two LCVPs following wake."[2] We anchored in Maalaea Bay, Maui, and the next day returned to Pearl Harbor.

Captain Arthur A. Ageton, Commander LST Flotilla 3, later commented: "Although ships were in all stages of repair, loading and logistics on 28 August, it was possible to complete repairs, complete loading, load LVT at Koko Head on 30 and 31 August, fire anti-aircraft practices, and have 20 of the 24 LSTs participate in rehearsal at Maui from 1 to 6 September. Two of the ships suffered serious breakdown and had to be returned early to the Navy Yard for repairs."[3]

On 5 September repairs on the bow ramp were completed, and we received orders to proceed to Kaneohe Bay,[4] on the east shore of Oahu, north of Kailua. Two days later we sailed to Maunalua Bay, near Koko Head, where we loaded LVT amphibious tanks.

Finally we started west toward the lands we'd read of in the papers— Kwajalein, Eniwetok, Tarawa, Guadalcanal, Tulagi, Saipan, Tinian. What would be next? This time we would be there, as participants.

We had barely passed the breakwater when the skipper tossed a battle plan the size of a Sears catalog onto the chart table. We took a look.

Yap? Where in the world is Yap?

Notes

[1]   LST 698 deck log, 2 September 1944

[2]   *Ibid.*

[3]   LST Flotilla 3 Action Report, 4 November 1944, covering landings on San Jose, Leyte, from 20 to 24 October 1944

[4]   In accordance with AdComPhibsPac secret dispatch 080249 (per LST 698 log, 8 September 1944)

8

Hundreds of Ships—
All Going to Yap?

As part of a large convoy, we cross the International
Date Line and anchor briefly in Eniwetok to receive fuel,
water, and fresh provisions, then head south to Manus and
Seeadler Harbor in the Admiralties

September 1944—As we sailed west from Pearl Harbor,[1] our immediate destination turned out to be Eniwetok, an atoll in the northern portion of the Marshall Islands. We were in a good-sized convoy of other LSTs, with a protective screen of a destroyer and half a dozen patrol craft (PCs) or subchasers (SCs). Such convoys were generally the rule once we entered regions closer to combat. The screen took positions fore and aft of our convoy and on either side.

Traveling in convoy, our chief communication among ships was through the hoisting of signal flags. The "corpen" flag, for example, denoted a change of course. The flags corpen, 2, 7, and 0 would indicate a change of course to 270 degrees (or due west).

Watches were assigned to the officers and enlisted men—often four hours on and eight hours off or perhaps four on and twelve off. A "dog watch" divided the 1600 to 2000 (4 to 8 p.m.) watch into two parts of two hours each, permitting those on watch to eat closer to 1800 and also to rotate the watches, so that no one would have the midwatch (midnight to 0400) more than his share.

Each watch was headed by one senior and one junior watch officer. (I was junior, because I had come to the ship directly from midshipman school instead of attending amphibious school like most of the officers and men.)

The watch officers were responsible for maintaining course and speed and keeping their ship in correct position in the convoy—usually 500 yards astern of the ship ahead in their column. They watched for signals from other ships, any changes in weather, sighting of aircraft, etc., and were required to notify the captain immediately of any of a hundred things that he should be apprised of.

Watch assignments were in addition to each person's assigned duties. As assistant navigator, it was my job (and the executive officer's) to know the ship's position at all times, keeping a running position on the current navigational chart and preparing charts for future use.

We carefully studied the invasion plan for Yap, which the captain had brought aboard at Pearl Harbor. This plan covered every aspect of the operation—preliminary bombardment by ships and planes, height of trajectory of ships' shells to protect the planes flying above them, the courses and times of arrival of all convoys taking part, specific landing points for all boats carrying personnel and weapons to the beach, the tasks of each unit, objectives and timetables for the whole operation.

I worked with Al Clingen, of Orange, N.J., our quartermaster, who drew in on the charts such points and special areas as "Green Beach A." Similarly, Bill Chapman, the communications officer, studied the communications plan and prepared to use any special codes. The gunnery officer examined anything related to his responsibilities, etc.

About eight days out from Pearl Harbor we crossed the International Date Line, longitude 180 degrees east *or* west from Greenwich, England. Today became tomorrow just like that. No ceremonies or anything.

"Out where the trade winds play, out where you lose a day . . . ."

A few days before reaching port, the mailbox began to fill up, and the officers again had to sit down at a table in the wardroom for censorship duties. This time it was something different. About half the crew must have gone into the same Honolulu photo shop. In letter after letter the sailors were sending home pictures of themselves, holding on their laps a hula girl in a grass skirt—the same girl in picture after picture!

Eventually Eniwetok came in view, just barely—little islands that rose only a few feet above the surface. The few palms we saw had been pretty well blown apart by bombardment before the atoll had been secured on 3 April 1944 by the 22nd Marine regiment.

Eniwetok is one of those countless Pacific atolls that resulted from centuries and centuries of coral deposits. Reefs connect Eniwetok's islands, which are arranged in a circle—roughly 20 miles north to south and 15 miles west to east. The water within is sufficiently shallow for ships to drop anchor. It made an enormous harbor, and we found ourselves in the midst of hundreds of ships. This made the tiny islands themselves practically invisible.

The harbormaster assigned our ship to a numbered anchorage set out like cookie cutter circles on the harbor chart. Most harbor operations were conducted from ships. We took on diesel fuel and water from tankers and then located a supply ship which furnished us with provisions. We were amazed at what we received—fresh meats, vegetables, fruit, and even watermelons and honeydews!

Our stay was brief. The next day we headed south toward Manus,[2] an island of the Admiralty group north of the eastern portion of New Guinea.

This leg of the journey took us about eight days, and it brought us south of the Equator. Such a crossing has traditionally provided an opportunity to initiate landlubbers who were crossing it for the first time. But in our case some half dozen men would have had to initiate 300 to 400 officers and men (including the army troops). They didn't take them on. We eventually crossed the equator eight times, and never a ceremony.

Looking back, I figured we had sailed roughly 6,000 miles from San Diego to reach Manus. We had left San Diego on 7 August and arrived at Manus on 5 October. This Pacific Ocean was BIG!

We entered Seeadler Harbor and suddenly saw hundreds and *hundreds* of ships—far more hundreds that we had seen in Eniwetok. All a part of the U.S. fleet.

They couldn't *all* be heading for *Yap!*

Notes

[1]   AdComPhibsPac secret dispatch 100337 (per LST 698 log, 10 September 1944)

[2]   CTF (Com Gr. 3 Phibs Pac) top secret dispatch 251914 (per LST 698 log, 26 September 1944)

9

Strategy Changes—
Timetable Moves Up

*High-level talks in London, Hawaii, and Quebec set
strategies and timetables; after Luzon carrier raids, Admiral
Halsey urges canceling some invasions and pushing assault
on Leyte ahead two months*

October 1944—While we were sailing from Pearl Harbor to
Eniwetok and then to Manus, big strategy changes were being made.
As a result, Yap was scratched as our invasion target.

High-level meetings had been held in June 1944 in London, in
July in Hawaii, in September in Quebec to determine the grand
strategy of Pacific operations against Japan. Admiral King and the
Navy favored bypassing the Philippines and invading Taiwan. General
MacArthur insisted on "liberating the Philippines and using Luzon
for the final or semifinal springboard to Japan," according to Historian
Samuel Eliot Morison.[1]

President Roosevelt had sailed to Pearl Harbor with Admiral
William D. Leahy, chief of staff to the Commander in Chief, in late
July, to confer with Admiral Nimitz and General MacArthur (who flew
in from the Southwest Pacific). MacArthur convinced the President

and Nimitz that "both national honor and sound strategy required the liberation of the Philippines before we went further."[2]

The Combined Chiefs of Staff drew up a timetable at the Quebec Conference, in September 1944:[3] In *September,* MacArthur would take Morotai and Nimitz Peleliu. *October:* Nimitz would take Yap in the Carolines, then Ulithi a few days later, then Talaud. *November:* MacArthur would occupy Sarangani Bay, Mindanao. In *December,* MacArthur and Nimitz would together invade Leyte.

That timetable lasted only a week. Admiral Halsey had conducted carrier raids on the Philippines, "steamed up to within sight of shore, pounded Japanese airfields, and destroyed the few Japanese planes that they encountered . . . Halsey sent a message via Nimitz to the Joint Chiefs of Staff, then sitting at Quebec . . . recommending that the Peleliu, Morotai, Yap and Mindanao operations be canceled, and that Pacific Fleet and Seventh Fleet make a joint assault on Leyte 20 October, two months ahead of schedule."[4]

The Joint Chiefs of Staff then sent directives to General MacArthur and Admiral Nimitz:

1. Admiral Wilkinson's Yap Attack Force, the XXIV Army Corps, then loading or at sea, to be assigned to General MacArthur to land at Leyte 20 October.
2. All shipping used in the Palaus operation, after unloading, to be sent to Southwest Pacific ports to help VII 'Phib lift General Krueger's Sixth Army to Leyte.
3. All fire support ships and escort carriers used in the Palaus operation to be assigned to Admiral Kincaid, Commander Seventh Fleet, to help cover Leyte.
4. Ulithi to be seized promptly, as an advanced fleet base.[5]

Some 738 ships were quickly assembled in the Central Philippines Attack Force. They consisted of "157 combatant ships, 410 amphibious types, 64 patrol, minesweeping and hydrographic types and 73 service types," according to Cinqpac Monthly Analysis for October 1944.[6]

Historian Morison reported that these were "fewer than those that took part in the invasion of Normandy in June, but mounting a heavier striking power. If we add the 18 fleet carriers, 6 battleships, 17 cruisers and 64 destroyers of the Third Fleet, this was the most powerful naval force ever assembled. But new records were being hung up by the Pacific Fleet every few months, and the one for Leyte would be equaled at Lingayen Gulf in January 1945 and surpassed off Okinawa in April."[7]

The operation was under the command of General Douglas MacArthur, Supreme Commander, Allied Forces, Southwest Pacific Area. Vice Admiral Thomas C. Kincaid headed the Seventh Fleet and Central Philippines Attack Force. The latter consisted of two separate task forces:

- **Northern Attack Force,** under Rear Admiral Daniel E. Barbey, staged at Hollandia, New Guinea, and landed its troops at the north end of Leyte Gulf off San Pedro Bay, just south of Tacloban.
- **Southern Attack Force,** under Vice Admiral T. C. Wilkinson, staged at Manus, Admiralty Islands, and brought its troops to the beaches near Dulag, about 12 miles to the south of the Northern Force.

The Northern Force had 471 ships, the Southern Force 267 ships.[8] Of the amphibious vessels, 152 were LSTs—97 in the Northern Force and 55 in the Southern Force.[9]

Our LST 698 was one of 24 LSTs in LST Flotilla 3, under Commander Arthur A. Ageton. This flotilla had sailed from Hawaii to Eniwetok, expecting to participate in the invasion of Yap. But when the invasion of Leyte was moved up from December to October, LST Flotilla 3 joined the Southern Force at Manus for the Leyte assault.

LST Flotilla 3 and LSM Division 15 together formed Task Unit 79.6.1, an LST-LSM transport unit, according to the LST Flotilla 3 Action Report of 7 November 1944:

> Due to exigencies of the service, LST Flotilla 3 (temporary) was put together hurriedly of ships from LST Flotillas 3, 5 and 16, and with group commanders from Flotillas 3 and 16. There

were very old ships in bad material condition and a large
proportion of very new ships with no combat and little sea-
going experience. [We were among the latter!] For example,
only eight of 24 LSTs had ever handled amphibious tractors
and tanks before the rehearsal. Some ships had beached only
once and then under ideal conditions."[10] [Our ship *had* beached
under a variety of conditions. See chapter 2.]

The original flotilla commander, Commander J. J. Graham, U. S.
Navy, had command from 17 to 28 August 1944, when he was
hospitalized. Commander Arthur A. Ageton, U. S. Navy, Commander
LST Flotilla 5, was immediately assigned to temporary command of
the flotilla and reported to ComPhibsGroupSix for duty that day for
the projected Yap invasion.

Our group commander, Lieutenant Commander Louis A. Drexler,
U.S.N., reported on 21 August 1944 and brought our new group of
LSTs from the mainland. This was his first experience in landing
craft.[11]

Many of the LSTs in the Northern Attack Force under Admiral
Barbey had rich backgrounds of service in such Southwest Pacific
invasions as Lae, Finschafen, Cape Gloucester, Admiralty Islands
(Manus and Los Negros), Biak, or Morotai under General MacArthur.

Eight of the 24 LSTs in our LST Flotilla 3, had served in the
Western Pacific in places like Kwajalein, Guam, and Saipan. Three of
these had seen action at Hollandia, New Guinea, with the Southwest
Pacific forces before joining the Western Pacific operations at Guam.
But the other 16 (including ours) were brand new.[12]

Notes

[1]   Morison, Samuel Eliot: *Two-Ocean War,* Little, Brown and Company, New
      York, 1963, 356-8

[2]   Morison, Samuel Eliot: *History of United States Naval Operations in World War
      II, Volume XII, Leyte, June 1940-January 1945,* Little, Brown and Company, New
      York, 1958, 10

[3]   Morison, *Two-Ocean War, op. cit.,* 357-8

4. *Ibid.*

5. Morison, *History, Vol. XII, op cit.,* 15

6. *Ibid.,* 113

7. *Ibid.*

8. Barbey, Daniel E.: *MacArthur's Amphibious Navy,* Naval Institute Press, Annapolis, 1969, 237

9. Morison, *op. cit.,* 415-420

10. LST Flotilla 3 Action Report, 7 November 1944, covering landings on San Jose, Leyte, from 20 to 24 October 1944, 3

11. *Ibid.*

12. *Dictionary of American Fighting Ships, Vol. VII,* James L. Mooney, editor, Naval Historical Center, Department of the Navy, Washington, D. C., various pages

10

Third Wave at Leyte; 3 Busy Days

LST 698 joins hundreds of ships sailing to Leyte, in the heart of the Philippines. In the third wave, our troops go ashore in amphibious tanks. We launch the LCT. Our LCVPs carry cargo and ammunition to the beach. We leave for Hollandia just in time to miss the Battle for Leyte Gulf

October 1944—For six days we remained in Seeadler Harbor, Manus, busily making trips to the base to procure additional supplies—and getting our first mail since we left Pearl Harbor.

The harbor, two degrees south of the equator, is 15 miles long and four miles wide. It had been wrested from the Japanese about six months earlier.[1] Two islands fit together to form the harbor—the larger, Manus, on the west and Los Negros on the east, separated by the tiny Lonio passage.

By October Manus had a whole city of Quonset huts loaded with supplies of all kinds. Referring to the "magnificent, deep, landlocked harbor," historian Samuel Eliot Morison remarked, "Far better as a base than Rabaul, and nearer to Japan, the Admiralties became one of the most important staging points in the last 15 months of the Pacific War."[2]

Hundreds and hundreds of ships were here, and more coming in each day. We recognized many we had spotted earlier in Eniwetok.

Signal lights flashed communications from one ship to another. Small boats, chiefly LCVPs (landing craft vehicle, personnel) ran all over the harbor carrying people and supplies.

The skipper was off the ship more than he was aboard, and so were many of the other skippers. (This was easily determined. Scanning the harbor we noted many "third repeater" pennants hoisted from the ships' yardarms, indicating, "The captain is ashore." One tiny LCI (landing craft infantry) managed to get a huge third repeater from a battleship. When hoisted, that meant the captain was *really* ashore!)

We spotted our skipper's boat returning. As it pulled alongside, he climbed briskly up the ladder, stepped onto the quarterdeck, and gave an order to the officer of the deck: "Set the special sea detail."

Other ships began to stir. Their "third repeaters" went down. Signal flags went up on LSTs all around us. The skipper quickly took his position on the conn, directly above the bridge, and I joined him. (Ken Saunders, the executive officer, was stationed in the gun tub in the ship's bow.)

Soon ship after ship hauled up its anchor and headed for the harbor entrance. We were under way for Leyte, in the heart of the Philippines.

As we left the harbor, each ship filed into its predetermined place in a formation of 24 LSTs and six LSMs (landing ships medium), five columns wide, flanked on each side and fore and aft by 23 LCIs (landing ships infantry). The screen included five destroyers, three PCs (patrol craft) and eight SCs (subchasers). Our LST Flotilla 3 commander, Commander Arthur A. Ageton, USN, was in the U.S.S. *Luce* (DD 522).[3] We were transporting assault troops of the 96th Infantry Division, with their LVPs (amphibious tractors) and equipment.

Here we were, a mighty convoy of LSTs sailing northwest on a quiet sea of blue. We re-crossed the equator, and the tropical sun passed nearly overhead at noon in its east-west path across the sky.

In the days that followed, we practiced drills and tactical exercises and stood general quarters. Various SCs and LCIs came alongside for fuel and water or to deliver guard mail. We transferred a private first class with acute appendicitis via LCI to the LST 118 (a hospital LST).[4]

We had lots of work to do. Al Clingen, the quartermaster, had pulled out the charts of Leyte Gulf and was drawing in with India ink the various beaches at Dulag, where we would send off the troops and supplies in amphibious tractors and our LCVPs. I was temporarily taken off the watch list in order to devote full time to navigation.

On the afternoon of the 19th, as we approached the entrance to Leyte Gulf, convoys were visible in every direction. At 1430 our convoy regrouped according to a plan, putting our five columns of LSTs into four columns and reducing the distance between the columns.

By late evening we had passed between the islands of Dinagat and Homonhon—just one of some 738 ships (including 152 LSTs) that passed through into Leyte Gulf that night. At 0330 we went into general quarters, all men at battle stations.

Through the night, I divided my time between the chart house and conn. Glenn Bavousett of Fort Worth, Texas, (or "Tex"), the radarman, and I kept close check on our position as we advanced, and the captain stayed almost continuously at the conn.

It was something like rush-hour traffic. At one time the ships slowed. We gained a bit on the ship ahead and seemed to be right under that ship's fantail. The single entry in the ship's 0400-0800 log was "steaming as before." We wondered when the action would begin.

At 0818 on 20 October, the log reported, we anchored in berth 22, LST Area William, about two miles from the beach. On command we began launching 15 LVPs (landing vehicles personnel) and three DUKWs (amphibious trucks or "ducks"). Officers and men of the 96th infantry disembarked into these amphibious personnel carriers and headed for the beach in the third wave. Flotilla Commander Ageton wrote:

> When halfway to the beach, the bombardment stepped up in tempo to what must have been the equivalent of a General Montgomery "serenade." The mortar ships and gunboats joined in with their specialized weapons. Although the smoke and dust were thick on the beach, we could see the landing beaches and immediate rear area were under a veritable hail of gunfire. It was the most impressive display of gun power I've ever seen. I was not greatly surprised when Colonel Turner, leader of the am-tanks in Tare Wave, reported by radio that the landing was virtually unopposed.[5]

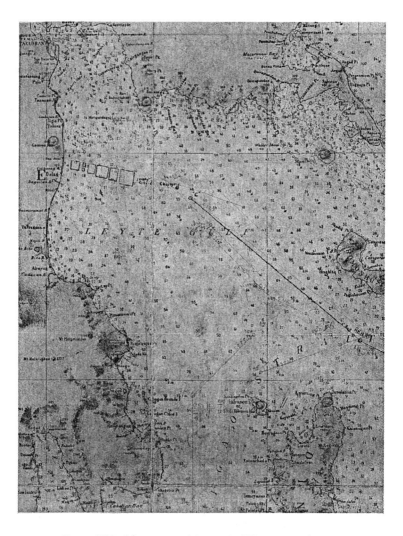

Some 738 ships entered Leyte Gulf between Dinagat and Homonhon (lower right) on the night of 19-20 October 1944. The Northern Force headed for predetermined positions in San Pedro Bay (upper left), while the Southern Force proceeded to positions off Dulag, about 15 miles to the south. *U. S. C. & G. S. 4719.*

At 0934 we got underway and in 40 minutes dropped anchor in LST Area Yoke, about five miles back from the beach. Shortly afterward we secured from general quarters.

We still had the LCT 898 (landing *craft* tank), which we took on in New Orleans in July, resting on our main deck—in fact, occupying a good part of that deck. The LCT was 117 feet long, with a 32-foot beam.[6] Our crew sometimes referred to it derogatively as a garbage scow. It could very well have become just that—a harbor vessel performing any number of harbor duties without ever going to sea.

But now the LCT's time had come. Our crew prepared to launch it, removing the rail along our port side and taking out some blocks. The ship was given a port list by pumping water and oil from starboard compartments to port side. Then a slight push, and it slid sideways neatly into the water. Our crew filled it with 2,200 gallons of fuel and 4,400 gallons of water.[7] Its skipper and his 12 men took over their ship and charged off into the wild blue yonder of Leyte Gulf. We gazed upon a great expanse of main deck that had lain hidden from us for months.

Since no space on the beach was available for beaching, we moved our LST two miles forward to Area X-ray to unload the remainder of our cargo. From time to time we went into general quarters but there was no action involving us. In the ship's log, Bill Chapman, who had the midwatch (midnight to 0400, 21 October) reported, "Spasmodic shelling and beachhead consolidation taking place."[8]

That next afternoon, we moved forward and anchored 1,000 yards off Orange Beach. The crew commenced unloading top-deck cargo into LCVPs. Commander Ageton reported:

> About 1420, observed mortar fire falling on LST beached, on LSTs anchored close to shore, and in vicinity of *Luce*. Seven LSTs were hit by mortar shells or damaged by close bursts. The mortar fire continued until about 1505, at which time gunfire from *Rocky Mount* registered on the enemy mortar locations at the foot of Catmon Hill and stopped it . . . In all, the unloading progressed very satisfactorily until 1420. After the mortar shelling, it was very difficult to get DUKWs and LVTs going again . . . [9]

LST after LST delivered its cargo of trucks, food, supplies, munitions, road-building equipment. With no docks or wharves in most areas, these ships charged bow-first right up onto the beach, avoiding transfer from ships to boats. *National Archives.*

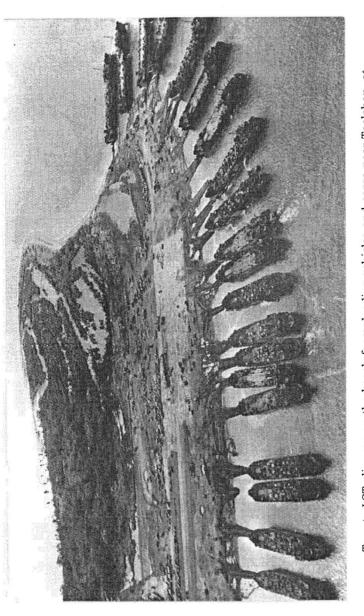

Twenty LSTs line up on the beach for unloading vehicles and cargo near Tacloban, at the northern end of Leyte Gulf. The gradual slope of this beach made it necessary to build earthen causeways out to the ships' bow ramps. *National Archives.*

The truck ramp (partly in bright sunlight) is lowered to allow vehicles on the main deck to go out through the bow doors. Earlier LSTs had an elevator, but the truck ramp installed on later ships permitted much faster loading and unloading. *Real War Photos.*

After the last vehicles emerged through the cavernous opening in the LSTs bow, the ramp was raised and it formed a seal where it joined the ship's bulkhead. The bow doors then closed, the ship retracted and another LST took its turn. *National Archives.*

Amphibious tanks, known as LVTs or Amphtracs, rolled out of the LSTs bow doors and churned through the sea to the beach, traveling through swamps or over rough terrain. *National Archives.*

During the enemy attack on the beach, Walter DeHaan, a fireman first class in one of our boat crews, was wounded in the left forearm by flying shrapnel.[10] It was not serious, but he was temporarily transferred to another ship for treatment. He was recommended for a Purple Heart. That was our only casualty.

That night all hands unloaded ammunition into the LCVPs. Over the next two days we unloaded the remainder of our cargo and provided fuel and water for a number of smaller ships which tied up alongside.

Historian Morison noted:

> The Leyte Gulf landings were easy, compared with most amphibious landings in World War II—perfect weather, no surf, no mines or other underwater obstacles, slight enemy reaction, mostly mortar fire . . . [On 20 October] Dulag was captured by the 7th Division around noon . . . Dulag and Tacloban airfields fell into American hands on 21 October, and the Army Engineers promptly went to work improving them . . . By midnight, 132,400 men and almost 200,000 tons of supplies and equipment had been landed by the assault echelons of the Northern and Southern Attack Forces, and most of the ships had departed.[11]

During the period from 20 to 24 October, personnel on eight of the 24 LSTs in LST Flotilla 3 received casualties. Five men were killed and 35 wounded[12] in the short encounter described by Commander Ageton.

On 24 October at 1100[13] we got underway for Hollandia, New Guinea.

What we didn't know at the time, and were startled to learn later, was that the landings at Leyte had set off one of the great air and sea battles of all time, the Battle for Leyte Gulf, 24-25 October 1944.

Notes

[1]   29 Feb to 3 Apr 1944. Barbey, Daniel L.: *MacArthur's Amphibious Navy*, Naval Institute Press, Baltimore, MD, 1969, 144-157

[2]   Morison, Samuel Eliot: *The Two-Ocean War,* Little, Brown and Company, New York, NY, 1963, 246

[3]   LST Flotilla 3 Action Report, Assault and Occupation of Leyte from 20-24 October 1944, 7

[4]   LST 698 deck log, 12 October 1944

[5]   LST Flotilla 3 Action Report, *op. cit.,* 41

[6]   Barbey, *op. cit.,* 361

[7]   LST 698 Deck Log, 20 October 1944

[8]   *Ibid.,* 21 October 1944

[9]   LST Flotilla 3 Action Report, *op. cit.,* p. 44

[10]   LST 698 Deck Log, *op. cit.*

[11]   Morison, *Two-Ocean War, op. cit.,* 369

[12]   LST Flotilla 3 Action Report, *op. cit.,* 68

[13]   In accordance with CTG 79 Secret Dispatch 230258, dated 23 October 1944, in Task Force 79.14.5, as noted in LST 698 Deck Log, 24 October 1944

11

The Naval Battle for Leyte Gulf

Where had the Japanese fleet been hiding? What brought them out? What was their plan? And the outcome?

October 1944—Three days before the Leyte invasion, on October 17, American minesweepers, sweeping the channel near Dinagat and the small islands at the opening of Leyte Gulf, had been sighted by a Japanese garrison, which passed the information on to the Japanese commander in chief. Immediately he ordered all Japanese vessels to get underway to execute their Sho-1 battle plan— and wipe out the American invasion forces on Leyte and our ships in Leyte Gulf.

The major elements of their fleet had not been seen since the Battle of the Philippine Sea in June. It turned out that some ships were in Japan's Inland Sea, but more were at Lingga Roads, near Singapore, where there were more plentiful supplies of oil. Now practically every available ship in the Japanese Navy was thrown into action.

They formed four forces to close in on Leyte. The Center Force and Southern Force were to come in from the west. The Southern Force was to pass north of Mindanao and through the Surigao Strait into Leyte Gulf, while the Center Force would steam through the Sibuyan Sea and San Bernardino Strait into the Philippine Sea north of Samar. The two groups would form a pincer movement against our operations in Leyte Gulf.

A Northern Group, from Japan, was to move down the east side of Luzon and serve largely as a decoy to lure our Task Force 38 away from the Leyte area. A second group from Japan would come in behind the Southern Force.

In four battles that ranged over some 800 miles, from the Palawan Strait in the southwest Philippines north of Borneo to the northern tip of Luzon off Cape Engaño, the Japanese lost a catastrophic portion of their fleet. Historian Samuel Eliot Morison described these epochal battles in great detail in Volume XII of his *History of United States Naval Operations in World War II.*[1] And in his single volume, *The Two-Ocean War,* he summarized the encounter thus:

> The four-part Battle for Leyte Gulf that followed [unloading of our amphibious vessels] comprised every type of naval warfare invented up to that time—heavy and light gunfire; bombing, strafing, rocketing and torpedoing by land-based and carrier-based planes; torpedo attacks by submarines, destroyers and motor torpedo boats. Every naval weapon but the mine was employed by both sides, and the Japanese introduced new and deadly air tactics. In every part the action was memorable and decisive, resulting in the destruction of the Japanese Fleet as an effective fighting force . . . [2]

And C. Vann Woodward, in *The Battle for Leyte Gulf,* says:

> Rarely in all naval history has a power staked so much upon one operation as the Japanese did in this, and rarely has any power suffered such an overwhelming defeat. Leyte Gulf was the last surface battle and the last naval engagement of any size in the war . . . After Leyte Gulf, our command of the sea was undisputed, save by land-based planes.[3]

It's hard to believe all this was going on without our even being aware of it, when we had been so close. One of the largest amphibious invasions in history had been followed by the greatest naval battle of all time. We participated in the one but were oblivious of the other, which did so much to make the landings successful. Why didn't it come off the way Japan's admirals expected?

- The Japanese were taken by surprise. They anticipated a U. S. invasion of the Philippines but not so soon. And they didn't know whether it would be Mindanao, Leyte, or even Luzon. Their ships near Singapore were 2,400 miles away and those in Japan 3,000 miles away. It took them a week to get to Leyte Gulf.
- By then most of our transports and LSTs were already out of the gulf.
- Communications from our planes and submarines informed our command quickly about advancing Japanese vessels, giving us time to deploy our ships to take them on.
- The number of Japanese planes was already limited. Some of their carriers carried no planes at all.
- And our American forces did a great job, individually and collectively.

Notes

[1] Morison, Samuel Eliot: *History of United States Naval Operations in World War II, Volume XII, Leyte: June 1944-January 1945,* Little, Brown and Company, New York, 157 *et. seq.*

[2] Morison, Samuel Eliot: *The Two-Ocean War,* Little, Brown and Company, New York, 1963, 370

[3] Woodward, C. Vann: *The Battle for Leyte Gulf,* Macmillan, New York, 1947, 12. Granted permission from Simon & Schuster, New York

12

Quiet Interlude, Sailing to Hollandia

More on what life is like aboard an LST. Church services,
good meals, going after rust, refueling smaller ships, bartering
for supplies as we cruise to Hollandia, New Guinea

October 1944—Let's take a moment to tell a bit more about day-to-day life on our LST, starting with the Sunday, October 15, before we entered Leyte Gulf.

We had both Catholic and Protestant services in the morning in the LCT, on our main deck. Both services were conducted by the Army. A Catholic army chaplain who was aboard had been holding mass every afternoon. Consequently the Catholics had a regular Catholic mass, and our Protestant service didn't have to be as ecumenical as usual. One of the soldiers gave the sermon. The four hymns sounded louder than usual, due either to a larger attendance or lustier hymns. This started a lot of church music running through my head.

On October 17 I had a full day. General quarters at five, then breakfast and a little rest before my 8 to 12 watch. In the afternoon I worked in the charthouse the whole time, studying charts and making changes and additions. Sandy and I handled star sights after supper, and then I had the 8 to 12 watch that night.

One of the infantrymen came down with appendicitis. Our wardroom had been equipped as an emergency operating room, with a large light over one of the tables, and we had an Army doctor on board, but we found it better to transfer the patient to another LST in our convoy, fitted out as a hospital ship. LCI 754 pulled alongside, we put the soldier over the side, and the LCI transferred him to the LST 118.[1]

We had an amateur hour, organized by the Army, but with both Army and Navy participating. Singing, harmonica playing and miscellaneous fun. Al Polarevic, a gunner's mate from Chicago, did some fancy tap dancing that won honors, a $10 prize.

On the day before the invasion we had special chow with ham and sweet potatoes, cake and ice cream. The cooks had saved ice for four days to make the ice cream. The two-layer cake was about 12 feet long (really a series of cakes), with frosting depicting our travels since San Diego. It was on display in the morning and hastily devoured at noon. The men got all they could eat. It was some job to feed as many as we had aboard (roughly 200 Army in addition to our crew of about 130 and a dozen officers), but the cooks did a good job.

During the four days we were in Leyte Gulf, everybody worked hard all through the day and well into the night. Watches cut into many of the night hours. General quarters interrupted either work or sleep.

When we got under way to leave Leyte, the water was very clear and blue, and it was not too warm. (Not exactly football weather, though!)

We began fall housecleaning. With the ship to ourselves, all hands went after rust spots, scraping them, putting on a bright yellow zinc chromate paint, and then painting everything in sight. Paint didn't last long on the metal surfaces, so the job was really needed.

Some of the ships that had been out the longest looked dull and rusty. Most of the LSTs had a camouflage pattern of light green, dark green, brown and gray. Our bulkheads were soon freshly painted in white, with the trim, baseboards and deck a dark green. It looked snappy, and once the work was done, the crew felt good to have their ship in good condition.

LCIs and other small ships often came alongside at sea. We put hoses across and transferred fuel and water to them without changing our course and speed. Our evaporators could make enough fresh water from salt water to take care of our own crew's needs, but we obtained fresh water from water barges each time we came into port. When we had a large number of troops aboard, we sometimes had to limit the use of fresh water for showers. But I think we did better than most ships our size.

On 30 October we arrived at Humboldt Bay, Hollandia, New Guinea (part of the Netherlands East Indies). This area had come into Allied control six months earlier, on 22 April 1944. After heavy bombardment by carrier planes and the Army Air Force, the Seventh Amphibious Force had made a three-pronged attack on Humboldt Bay, Tanamerah Bay, 30 miles to the west, and Aitape, about 120 miles east. Little opposition had been encountered. Admiral Daniel Barbey reported that with 217 ships, the forces had landed 79,800 Army and Army Air Force personnel, 50,000 tons of supplies, 232 Army boats, and 3,000 vehicles in the first three days.[2]

The afternoon that we arrived, a number of us went ashore. One of our priority missions was to procure mail, the first since we left Manus.

It was great to hear from Fran again. I received letters as recent as October 8 but also got letters dating back as far as July 16 and 17—letters that apparently just missed me in Panama and Pearl Harbor.

Hollandia was an amazing place. Plain wood buildings, many still under construction. Dirt roads with big mud puddles. At the post office, mail sacks were piled to the ceiling—hundreds of sacks for the various ships in the harbor. We felt lucky to get anything at all out of the place, but they managed to find three bags for us (one containing only piles of forms from Washington).

I laughed when my sister Helen wrote that she was going to the grocery early in the morning, because she heard they had sugar and butter. I was thinking of our own butter situation during the past week. We finally ran out, but not for long. We got some butter from an LCI in trade for some loaves of bread. Who knows what the LCI traded to get the butter in the first place, or how many times it had been traded altogether!

Ralph Hart's father wrote that the cigarette situation was so acute in St. Louis that he was considering smoking a pipe. Here our stock had sometimes run low enough so that it had to be rationed, but it had never run out.

We did have a soap shortage. Our last supply depot had nothing but P & G laundry soap. Even that would get by in a pinch. Every man dug into his private hoards (including my two little bars from the hotel in New Orleans). We hoped to make out better here.

November 1st was a big day for getting mail. Myron Bark of Tarentum, Pa., our mailman, came back with one sack of mail containing chiefly newspapers *and* the cookies Fran had sent me goodness knows how many months ago. The package was still all in one piece, but that's all you could say for it. The can had been bashed in as if it had been under a 20-ton crane all the way across the Pacific. As for the cookies, anything could be a treat over here. They weren't exactly in the best shape, but the raisins had kept them surprisingly fresh.

We knew there must be more mail than that, because we had seen so many sacks of it. And I had heard of one ship's getting several sacks of packages. So I asked Tex Bavousett to come with me. We jumped into a boat and went over to the post office to see what we could do.

(Tex Bavousett, a radarman from Dallas, was about 18, a big kid, curly haired, very good-natured, a nice fellow to have around. Operating the radar, he was at the other end of the voice tube when I was on the conn.)

We got permission to go behind the counter, where the mail sacks were arranged in big, long piles. All the sacks for LSTs in the 600s were in two great piles. Tex and I began looking at the tags. We found one sack after another, and in a few minutes we had pulled out 11 big sacks! We really surprised Coxswain Jack Costa of Bristol, R.I., and the other two fellows in the boat crew. You should have heard the cheers when we pulled up alongside the ship!

The mail took about an hour to sort. We hauled it all into the wardroom and about 20 men pitched in. We got another big batch of letters, but a great portion of it was newspapers and packages.

Fran sent me a copy of the National Geographic which contained an article on LSTs. It showed many of the things I had wanted to describe to her. There were no pictures of the bridge or officers' country, where I put in most of my time, but it showed what the inside of a tank deck looked like, how they set an LCT on the main deck, and how they eventually launched it at its destination.

How great it was to get that mail!

Notes

[1]   LST 698 deck log, 12 October 1944

[2]   Barbey, Adm. Daniel E.: *MacArthur's Amphibious Navy,* Naval Institute Press, Annapolis, 1969. (Hollandia is discussed in pp. 158-184)

13

We Explore Humboldt Bay

We discover a thatched-roof village and natives diving
for starfish; a Japanese storage dump (hastily abandoned);
banana and papaya trees

November 1944—The region of New Guinea around Humboldt Bay was quite beautiful, with steep green hills on all sides. The vegetation was rich. The weather was comfortable most of the time, but in the bright mid-day sun it got plenty hot. After all, it was just two degrees south of the equator.

We went sightseeing. After doing a few errands, Monty and I took the boat around into a corner of the bay to a native village. There we stopped, wandered through, and made a few trades with the natives.

The whole village, of perhaps 100 thatched-roof huts, was built on the water, with a pier running down the center and planks leading off to each of the huts. The natives were dressed almost any way—some of the men in Army shirts or undershirts, some of the women with cloth wound around them, the kids completely bare. Some of the older women were bare above the waist, showing thin, droopy breasts and tattoos on their shoulders and arms. The young maidens were discreetly covered.

The chief items of trade were fish spears, about six feet long, and bows and arrows. Some of the natives understood a few words of English and seemed well accustomed to the business of trading. The children practically lived in the water and at the slightest provocation would jump in. They dove for pennies or for starfish lying on the bottom.

The first boy who produced a starfish got a nickel for it, and it wasn't long before every kid in the village was diving for starfish. As we were leaving, one kid ran up to us with half a dozen. There was no sale. The boys could throw them back and wait for the next guy, though.

The starfish, I thought, was one of the funniest objects you could imagine. They had five points and were six to eight inches in diameter and quite thick. In water they had a series of what look like valves running along the bottom of each of their five arms. When they were out of water, these valves closed up and shrank back in. We heard that they fall apart when they're dry unless properly preserved. We put some in a bucket of water to bring them back to the ship.

No one would ever see such a village on a Cook's tour. However, it was far from untouched by civilization. One of the leading citizens, wearing a shirt and slacks, had a billfold with Dutch currency in it. Still, the village existed for itself, and not for the tourist trade.

We continued our journey back into the bay and tied up to a pier along a clearing. We found various storage dumps used by the Japanese during their time here. (Many had been set afire.) We discovered sacks of rice and barley, large tins of cocoa, tin cans probably containing fish, lots of packages of cigarettes, and writing tablets like the one I used for writing home to Fran. They seemed to be very well supplied for a long stay, but they must have departed in a hurry when the bombs started to come in.

While some of the fellows were concerned with this booty (the cigarettes and writing paper), Orlando Gonzales and I went on a banana hunt. Gonzales was Cuban, but hailed from Brooklyn—a member of one of the boat crews. He saw a big hock of bananas in a tree and shinnied up to get them. Just as he was nearly within reach, the tree toppled over from his weight and down he came, very gently, with the bananas!

They were green, but we hung them from the ceiling of my wardroom, waiting for them to ripen. We also found papayas by the score. We picked some of the largest and brought these back, too. Orlando and I thought we could have a feast when the bananas and papayas got ripe! My room looked (and smelled) like a fruit store!

The papayas were great. But unfortunately, the bananas became a home for worms long before they were ripe. We had to give up on them. The starfish didn't do any better.

We decided not to go into the produce business.

14

We Carry Air Force Troops to Leyte

At Biak we bring aboard Air Force troops and vehicles.
Time for a swim and a hatful of seashells. Six American
girls in swimsuits. At Leyte we beach in San Pedro Bay.
Dugout canoes. One-man Japanese air "raid"

November 1944—We hoisted anchor and got under way for Biak, about 325 miles to the northwest of Hollandia. Biak was the largest of the Schouten Islands, off the northwest coast of New Guinea. It had been the scene of heavy fighting in June of 1944.

After getting into the open sea, we had two hours of general quarters for target practice. Our men were getting good—they shot down two towed sleeves. Bill Eklund and I had the watch from 1200 to 1600, so I was on the conn most of the day. My forehead later felt a little sunburned. That sun really burned when we were out in it a long time, even though we tried to keep under the canvas awning-roof.

I wore gray pants and shirt, with collar open and sleeves rolled up. I almost never wore a hat except ashore or on O.O.D. watch in port, when I had to carry a .45. According to "Navy Regs," the Officer of the Deck in port "shall wear white gloves and carry a binocular." In wartime he rolled up his sleeves and packed a pistol.

66

Two days later we beached at Bosnik, on the southeast side of Biak, and began loading vehicles. We took aboard 29 officers and 255 men of the 5th Air Force.[1] Later we loaded lumber and small arms.

A busy day ended with some fun. I got an early start with the 0400 to 0800 watch. Then we had the "special sea detail," which kept me on the conn most of the time until we beached. Later I walked up the beach a short distance and saw some fellows swimming. I recognized one of the men from our ship. He and I decided we'd take a swim. So we pulled off our clothes and went in, without bothering with swimming suits. The beach was sandy, and the water was perfect—my first swim since Hawaii. We found coral a short distance out but could swim over it.

After that I wandered up and down the beach. I saw the remains of a Japanese landing craft, about the size of an LCM, next thing larger than our LCVPs. One fellow found the barrel of a gun.

I started picking up seashells and ended up with a whole hatful of them. I had to be careful, because just as I got ready to pick up a shell, it would suddenly start to walk away.

When I got back to the ship, I washed the shells and decided to send them home to Fran. Eventually she mounted them in a ring which we used as a centerpiece or around a lamp.

It had been very comfortable recently—not too hot. Surprisingly we hadn't had any weather equal to a real Chicago heat wave since we had been in the Pacific.

Election returns were sparse but we learned that Roosevelt had won again. At least we didn't have to stay up all night to learn the returns. We got our reports in the afternoon of the following day. I decided I'd have to wait until I got my *Time* for a tabulation by states.

Our chief source of news was the Philippine Hour, which came on at 1800 and originated in Australia. It gave about ten minutes of news of the Pacific theater and about five minutes of European war news, then music, normally American recordings.

We sailed a short distance to an anchorage in Mios Woendi Lagoon, Palaido Island, just south of Biak.

We had some excitement while at anchor. Word passed like lightning and in a few seconds all hands were topside, along the rail. An Army motor launch passed by, a few yards from the ship, exhibiting six, yes, six American girls in swimming suits, waving and smiling to the men! Later, when I was on shore, I saw them again, passing slowly by a group of PT boats. They were going through the same act and must have been having fun, in a place where a woman is someone you write letters to and look longingly at pictures of.

These must have been Army nurses, stationed nearby. The Army officers told us of the private wire they had between their officers' quarters and the nurses' home, and how they were forced to become almost civilized again, and not run around naked when they felt so inclined. (This was several miles from the beach on Biak where I had gone swimming the other day. There, I guess, civilization had not yet struck.)

We hauled anchor on 9 November for our return trip to Leyte Gulf, in the Philippines, taking departure from Mios Woendi Lagoon at 1801. We were assigned position 6 in a column, with the OTC (Officer in Technical Command) in *LST 917* in position 1.[2]

Suddenly at 2015 our ship veered left at a 45-degree angle while the rest of the convoy continued on its straight course. Ray Kennedy and I were the watch officers on the conn. Ray hollered down to the helmsman, who yelled back that he couldn't do a thing about it. The steering engines would not respond.

It turned out that the steering engine room was next to the ship's laundry, and the laundry tubs had overflowed and put the steering engines out of business. For the next several hours 10 or 12 men had to tug and pull the steering cables by hand to put the ship back on course and hold it there until the steering engines were dried out and repaired!

Next morning our LSTs merged into Echelon L-12, again part of LST Flotilla 3.[3] We traveled with them to our destination.

The papayas from Hollandia were getting ripe, and were quite a prize. They seemed to be ripening one by one. When they looked ripe, I put them in the refrigerator and told Gonzales. We split 50-50. Half a melon was more than one could eat, so we rationed our respective halves among our friends. (Our steward's mate, George Hickman, good politician that he was, once angled sections from each of us!)

This was a rolling voyage. The dinnerware didn't fly around, but it was still pretty rough. The victims this time seemed to be the Army. Only a handful of our sailors appeared to be troubled with seasickness.

Many of the Army officers had returned recently from vacations in Australia. We obtained a lot of information from them. It was hard to think that the nearest drug store or taxicab was that far away.

We had some excellent Australian bacon—thick, lean pieces like Canadian bacon. I made a couple of toasted bacon sandwiches that were great! Some ersatz eggs received no accolades.

The Army officers made many comments about how good our bread was. It was always fresh. It toasted well and had a slightly homemade flavor. The Army's bread, they said, was tough, had crust half an inch thick, and was usually burned. We gave credit to our baker, Roland Cote of Manchester, N.H., about 19 years old. His cakes and cinnamon rolls were really a treat.

After we entered Leyte Gulf, we sailed north to San Pedro Bay, a few miles north of where we had been on our first visit to Leyte. We beached on Yellow Beach and unloaded troops, trucks and dry cargo. We remained on the beach till morning, then pulled off and dropped anchor near our previous anchorage off Catmon Hill.

The bay was full of outrigger canoes, and several of these came up alongside our ship. They didn't have much to offer—a few bananas, two chickens, some eggs, and big wads of Japanese money. They wanted only one thing—clothes. I obtained another piece of Japanese currency in trade for two old skivvy shirts. The Filipinos were shrewd dealers. Even though the Japanese money had no value, they passed it out sparingly, because they found that it was much in demand as souvenirs.

These canoes were dugout style, boarded up at the ends. Bamboo pieces ran crosswise fore and aft, supporting heavy bamboo members, reaching about four feet out on each side of the boat.

The most amazing boat carried, by actual count, 27 men, women, children and babies, in all manner of costumes, from GI shirts to wide, conical Oriental hats. Two women had umbrellas to keep the sun away. This canoe was rowed by about 12 oarsmen. The paddles had round blades at the end, about a foot in diameter. In tow behind all this was an empty canoe, about a third the length of the first, like an emergency lifeboat.

The Filipinos looked bright and spoke amazingly good English. Someone yelled down, "You got any whisky down there?" and a native yelled back, "No, we do not have any," and grinned. They seemed happy about having the Americans around. They were getting more to eat and a few clothes on their backs.

We had a strong rain, and I got really soaked! I took a warm shower and put on dry clothes, and that made me feel good. I felt sorry for those Army fellows on shore who were often unable to enjoy such luxuries. They hated to leave our ship to start roughing it on the beach.

At 1758 on 16 November we got under way, returning to Hollandia, New Guinea, in task unit 78.2.34.[1]

Suddenly, after we had taken our position in the convoy of returning ships, we were startled to see a small Japanese plane, resembling a Piper cub, flying low, perhaps 200 feet, between our column and the column to our left. We saw the Japanese insignia, and some claimed they saw the Japanese pilot, with a mustache.

Our log reported, "1850 commenced firing at enemy plane. Expended 16 rounds of 40mm H.E.T. ammunition."[5] He flew blithely away and was soon out of sight at our rear.

Obviously we didn't get him, but it was enough "action" to qualify all aboard for a second star in our Philippine invasion ribbon—the first for being in Philippine waters 30 days or more (which we would complete after we invaded Lingayen in January), the second for "participating in enemy combat." Sort of!

We continued our journey, and at 2343 passed Desolation Point, Dinagat Island. We took departure from Leyte Gulf and headed once more for Hollandia.

Notes

[1] LST 698 deck log, 7 November 1944

[2] *Ibid.* 9 November 1944

[3] *Ibid.*, 10 November 1944

[4] *Ibid.*, 16 November 1944

[5] *Ibid.*

15

Hard Work—and Little "Meatball"

*Returning to Hollandia, many chores for many hands. A
bit about Stubby Green. We acquire a little dog and name him
Meatball. And when we reach port, we hit the mail jackpot*

November 1944—On our return trip from Leyte to Hollandia
we had a busy ship. A dozen different activities in a dozen different
places.

Some of the men scraped off rust and painted the main deck.
Others repainted the light gray parts of the camouflage on the
deckhouse. The bosun's mates rigged an awning on the navigation
bridge, forward of the wheelhouse.

And Stubby Green, Beach and Alexander, the shipfitters (officially
Vernon Green of Steubenville, Ohio, Richard Alexander of Calvert
City, Ky., and James Beach of Baltimore, Md.) had been busy welding.
They installed ladders from the navigation bridge to the signal bridge,
putting a stairway-type ladder on the port side where a straight iron
ladder had been, and putting the straight ladder aft, where the other
ladder had been.

They had also installed portholes in the officers' country, with tops
of used 40-mm ammunition cans. These had airtight, watertight covers
and, when opened, provided light and fresh air. Yet the portholes could

be sealed up instantly at night when we were blacked out while underway. In port, blackouts were generally considered unnecessary.

Whenever there was something to fix, they called on Stubby Green. He was one of the hardest-working fellows on the ship. One minute he was doing carpentry work, and the next he was running around in a welder's mask. Goodness knows what other ships did without Stubby. He was one of a kind.

He was impetuous, a live wire, and spoke at the top of his high-pitched voice. They took him off the watch list. He was one of the few who kept too busy to stand watches. But earlier, on our trip to Panama, he had been on watch with us and we just about split laughing at his hollering down the voice tube to Tex Bavousett, the radarman. There was a nurse aboard the transport ahead of us, and he'd yell, "Hey, Tex, what's the distance to the nurse?"

Stubby was quite a guy for acquiring anything he might need, and he'd come back to the ship with old chains, cable, bits of scrap metal. He and Alexander once brought a Japanese bicycle aboard. The bike had rubber tires, rubber handle grips, was complete in every way, and it ran. It was quite a trophy. You should see how Stubby polished it up!

Somehow we acquired a little brown puppy named Meatball. He came aboard with the Army, along with three other dogs, two cats and a duck. Then the Army left, and next morning we discovered Meatball the minute it was light, running across the main deck. He half ran and half jumped—really covered the ground.

Meatball was in the wardroom after breakfast. Next I saw him in the wheelhouse. Then I looked up toward the bow and saw him running across the truck ramp. While I was on watch, someone brought him up to the conn, and later I saw him back on the fantail.

Everybody claimed him, and he got around enough so that in the course of the day everyone got to pet him. I understand that one day he was given five baths! Various people presumed he needed one and took it upon themselves to do the job. No one seemed to know how we got him away from the Army. Some said the fellow who owned him gave him to us. Others said treachery was used—but we never found anyone who would admit it. (Oh, yes. It was not a he anyhow. It was a she!)

On Sunday I attended the church service. Our quartet sang "The Old Rugged Cross" and we read the 19th psalm. It was not much of a service, but it succeeded in bringing me right back to Wilmette. The quartet consisted of Lynn Martin, our yeoman from Houston, Mo.; George Hickman, steward's mate from Marion Station, Md.; Paul Gentry, a cook from Shelbyville, Tenn.; and Morris Gee, of Bedford, Ind.

We had the service forward on the truck ramp, in the shade of the gun tubs. It was cool, and the sky was blue almost up to the time it rained. In the midst of the service Meatball let out a couple of yelps. It reminded me of babies being baptized on communion Sunday.

Meatball came into the wardroom and the Captain offered her some chicken skin. She took it between her feet on the deck. The Captain decided she had better eat out in the passageway, so the meat was placed on a plate in the hall. A minute later, though, Meatball came back into the wardroom with the meat in her mouth and proceeded to eat it on the wardroom deck.

We had many beautiful sunsets. I described one of them in a letter to Fran: "The white clouds seemed to be piled fluff upon fluff, miles deep, with reflected light setting off various sides of them. The sky was blue, red, yellow, and even green, with edges of darker clouds fringing the horizon. And as we watched the western sky for Venus to appear, we saw the thin sliver of a brand new moon."

We had also seen porpoises again, jumping out of the water so that we could see just their heads, then their tails.

We reached Humboldt Bay on 22 November and hit the jackpot on mail. I received 17 letters from Fran, 11 letters from others, and three early Christmas packages.

16

Eight Men in a Boat—Learning

*In Hollandia we have a Thanksgiving feast, anti-
aircraft target practice, ship maneuvers, a rough boat trip.
We head for Finschhafen, New Guinea, and find offshore
islands whose positions don't match the charts*

November 1944—We learned a lot about seamanship and small
boat handling in one eventful day. We were in Humboldt Bay
(Hollandia, New Guinea) from 22 November to 4 December, busy
again doing in-port details in preparation for our next assignment.

But first some other happenings in port. On 23 November,
Thanksgiving Day. I wrote to Fran: "Our Thanksgiving Day was a
genuine festive occasion, but it was hard to think of the day particularly
as Thanksgiving. We had a fine meal—turkey, sweet potatoes,
cranberries, olives, and both pumpkin pie and a big dish of ice cream.
We were really stuffed, in true Thanksgiving style. However, it was just
our luck to have to move our ship alongside a tanker in the morning
to take on fuel, so we sat down for dinner about 45 minutes late. (You
can imagine the cooks' thoughts!) And then we had to return to our
anchorage in the afternoon."

We worked on charts the following day. Al Clingen (of Orange,
N.J.) and Rodney Spencer (of Madison, Wis.), our quartermasters,

and I tackled a big bunch of charts we had just received from Washington. Up to now I had had to beg for charts at chart depots, trying to fill shortages in our list. We never knew where we'd be going next or what charts we'd need. This brought back my acquisitive instinct, recalling when, as a boy, I used to collect road maps. My eyes would have popped to see such collections of charts as these, used by navigators at sea.

Some of the charts were really beautiful—from British or Dutch or German sources of 1873, 1893 or 1912. Others had been "borrowed" from the Japanese. We found that many remote areas had inadequate charts. Imagine the job of the Hydrographic Office when you think that every mile of coastline must be accurate, every mountain peak exactly in its place, every sounding correct, so that vessels will not go aground.

A new ensign, Albert Toll, from Philadelphia, reported for duty on 26 November. Washington sent him here for duty on the *698*, and he just showed up. He had been on his way since mid-October. We now had 12 officers. He looked like a good fellow—a graduate of Penn State, class of '41, and a chemical engineer in Ohio. He went to officer indoctrination school at Princeton, and this was his first assignment.

The ship tied up to ours had a movie, Rita Hayworth in *Cover Girl*, in Technicolor. It was pleasant under the stars—real stars, not the kind on the ceiling of a theater back home. The half moon made the screen a little faint. Movies did quite a job to provide entertainment out here. A good many ships in the harbor had projectors, but only flag LSTs were provided with them. We hoped to obtain one eventually.

I received from Fran a box of Christmas cards which she had addressed for me from my list. With the afternoon free, I got busy and wrote notes on all of them. It was 28 November, and they were all ready to mail!

We took the ship out onto the ocean for anti-aircraft target practice. Half the men thought they were pretty good shots. They knocked down another towed sleeve. Those on the other guns became determined to knock a sleeve down too, and they griped when the ship just ahead of us hit the sleeve and they didn't get another chance to shoot.

On another day we took the ship out on maneuvers. We practiced coming alongside another ship while underway, following zigzag patterns, etc. We had done that sort of thing at Panama City, Fla., on our shakedown cruise, but this was more advanced and more concentrated. I was on the conn much of the day.

The next day we had a two-and-one-half degree list to starboard in order to paint the port hull as far below the rusty water line as possible. The chief created the list by merely filling some starboard ballast tanks. We had to walk uphill to get to the port side.

Another day, what started as a simple boat trip to the base in an LCVP soon made us feel about as salty as New England fishermen. Bill Chapman, Myron Bark (gunner's mate and mailman) of Tarentum, Pa., a pharmacist's mate, the four men in the boat crew and I started out for the post office landing. We had various missions, to obtain certain naval publications, mail, medical supplies, and a few charts. It had just stopped raining, and we were in our rain gear, because the boat was wet.

We hadn't gone more than 100 yards before we saw that we were bucking a sea. And much of the sea was splashing into the boat. We charged on, getting an occasional lashing from the salt spray, which we rubbed out of our eyes and licked off of our lips.

Then we discovered that the bilge pumps were not working. The water in the bottom of the boat began to push up the floor boards, and soon planks, lines, and everything on deck started floating in three or four inches of water.

Bill Chapman took the wheel, the motor mac (machinist's mate) began pumping with the hand pump, and the rest of us started bailing with buckets and a large tin can. I could see why the Navy gave us all those deep knee bends in the gym program. It was down, scoop, up, out; down, scoop, up, out until whooie! I could still feel it in my legs the next morning.

Well, we managed to bail faster than the water came in, so we finally got to the base. While we were on shore, the fellows in the boat crew were able to hoist the boat up on the davits of a nearby LST, and they cleared out all the seaweed and foreign matter in the drain. So when we got back to the boat, everything was fine.

However, the water was still plenty rough, and darkness had set in. (It got dark here at 5:30 all year around.) But when we headed the other direction, the waves didn't bother us. And the pump kept the boat dry. When we got back to the ship, the sea was still too rough for us to hoist the boat onto the davits or even to tie it up alongside. We had to secure it by a line and let it drift off the fantail.

In this fairly open bay, the boat rocked from one side to the other. But there was something about these LCVPs that made me feel safe. Each time we rolled way over, we came right back. It must be impossible to tip the things over. I decided that the bilge pump is an important item! How good it felt to get back to the ship and into dry clothes.

At our Sunday church service, the quartet sang "Silent Night." But somehow it was hard to feel Christmas coming yet. Without store windows, Christmas trees for sale, and children getting excited—and particularly without snow. I wished I could be home with Fran this Christmas!

We pulled out of Humboldt Bay and took an eastbound course, heading for Finschhafen, at the eastern end of New Guinea.

On the second day out, we were in sight of land all day, cruising along the north coast of New Guinea. That made the trip more interesting. However, from the navigator's standpoint it had been something of a headache, because the small offshore islands were not where they were supposed to be, according to our charts. Imagine islands that are in truth four or five miles from their charted positions!

This showed how sketchily some of these remote areas of the world had been charted. One thing seemed certain. When the war was over, we'd have much more complete knowledge of the geography of our world.

We arrived in Finschhafen on 8 December, wondering who would be our next passengers and where we would take them.

17

We Take on Medics, Ambulances

At Finschhafen we drive around a big base to get supplies.
The Red Cross serves free lemonade. We beach and take on
19 officers and 262 men of the 108th Medical Battalion,
33rd Infantry, with their white ambulances

December 1944—We beached at Finschhafen, on the eastern end of New Guinea, on 8 December and found streets with such names as East 39th Street, West 63rd Street, and East 42nd Street.

Finschhafen had been captured by the Seventh Amphibious Force on 22 September 1943 with little opposition, only six days after the capture of Lae, about 100 miles down the coast. We had not been the first to find problems with the navigation charts. Admiral Daniel E. Barbey related:

> The movement of the various groups of ships to Finschhafen took place according to plan, a creditable performance since the charts we used were 11 miles in error.[1]

Like all such tropical bases, including the new ones in the Philippines, truck and jeep traffic kept to the left.

Lou Miller and I hooked a ride in a jeep. Or rather, an MP voluntarily flagged it down (that seemed to be his duty) to get us to the naval base several miles down the road. The jeep happened to be going only to the next gas station (large tanks 10 feet up in the air, using the gravity system), so we piled out and waited by the roadside. In a few minutes a big truck driven by a soldier slammed on its brakes, and it turned out to be the *698's* Ensign Bill Eklund of Austin, Tex., with shipfitters Stubby Green and Richard Alexander, on their way to get oxygen and acetylene.

So we jumped on the truck with the rest. We barreled along at a terrific rate, down the left-hand side of the road. We always seemed to miss by an eyelash the traffic in the opposite direction, which always managed at the last minute to veer over and pass us on the *right*. I was glad these fellows were used to driving on the left, because you'd expect someone new to pull over to the wrong side!

We passed endless units—an air base here, a quartermaster unit there, a mess kitchen, a church, a hospital, one thing after another. A baseball park seemed more carefully graded than you'd find in Chicago. The way the Army moved in, with its Quonset huts and trucks and jeeps, you'd expect them to become firmly established. Yet all of this could be loaded up and moved to more advanced bases.

Eventually we rumbled back to the ship, backed the truck right up to the bow doors, and rolled in the oxygen and acetylene.

Next day I found myself borrowing a jeep myself. I had to go down to the Australian chart depot on another of my chart collecting trips. I didn't have any idea where to go, so I hooked a ride in a jeep down to the Naval Supply Depot. When I asked a lieutenant for directions, he asked me if I had transportation. "No," I said, "I've done all right using my thumb, though." "Why don't you borrow my jeep?" Just like *that!*

So I piled in, looked around, found the ignition and starter, and *zing!* There I went, down the left-hand side of the road.

I drove several miles, and it's lucky I had the jeep, because there were so many different activities, some with big signs, others, like the chart depot, poorly marked. I went too far and ran into a huge Army warehouse area. I asked six people and finally got started in the right direction. Returning on the road I had been on, I saw the sign, turned down a side road toward the waterfront, and came to a neat, little thatch-roofed building. That was it. All of the partitions in the building were made of the same thatched material—about the only resemblance I had seen to the South Seas that we saw in movies.

The Australians were very pleasant, and I got most of the material I wanted. The Americans, Australians, and Dutch had access to each other's charts and navigational information. Five successive charts in our cruise from Hollandia were Australian, Dutch, American, British, and German.

We saw more natives here, along the roadside, than anywhere we had been except the Philippines. All had fuzzy, woolly hair. The most common clothing for men or women was a knee-length skirt, bright red if possible. We didn't see so many women. The ones we did see were bare to the waist like the ones in *National Geographic.*

There were various nurses and WACs here. It took no more than five minutes after we beached to discover a nurses' camp about 800 yards up the beach. The binoculars got plenty of use.

The Red Cross women offered free lemonade. Later we saw three of them drive past our ship in a jeep. I was surprised that our boatswain's mate didn't direct them to drive right in through the bow door.

It was 10 December, and my mind wandered to Christmas. Back home we were getting into the spirit, with the first Christmas cards, huge crowds in stores, and greater excitement with each day. Would we begin to feel that spirit soon? We knew that Christmas songs were all over the radio dial back home. How many of them would we hear out here? (We had a Christmas album we'd been saving.)

Our ship beached two miles south of Cape Cretin, where we took on as passengers the 108th Medical Battalion, 33rd Infantry, with 19 officers and 262 men, their vehicles and equipment. This included a fleet of white ambulances with big red crosses on top.

When we pulled off the beach, we anchored just offshore. We went swimming off the bow doors, with the ramp lowered to the water's edge. The water was fine. Since the ship swung on its anchor according to the tide or current, sewage and refuse were swept past the stern.

Thus the water at the bow was clear, provided there were not too many ships in the harbor.

Miller and I went over to a movie at an outdoor theater on the hospital grounds. We heard giggling behind us from nurses in the audience. The movie wasn't much—*Two Yanks Abroad,* with Dennis O'Keefe. In the middle of the picture it began to rain, and many took shelter under the eaves of the recreation hall. But the movie went right on. When we got back, our ship sounded like a dance hall, with music on the P.A. system for the men who stayed aboard.

We sailed out of Finschhafen on 11 December in Task Unit 76-4-12, with the Officer in Technical Command located on LST 917. We were bound for Morotai, an island in the Netherlands East Indies.

Notes

[1] Barbey, Daniel E.: *MacArthur's Amphibious Navy,* Naval Institute Press, Annapolis, 1969. (Finschhafen is discussed on pp. 88-96)

18

What a Time for an Appendectomy!

Calm waters, good equipment, and 19 physicians aboard make this surgery an easy task as we carry a Medical Battalion from Finshhafen, New Guinea, to Morotai, Netherlands East Indies

December 1944—It was a long cruise westward along the north coast of New Guinea and up to a little island named Morotai, in the Netherlands East Indies. We crossed the equator for the sixth time, returning, just barely, to the Northern Hemisphere.

This time we carried a medical unit, doctors and corpsmen of the 108th Medical Battalion. Our main deck and much of our tank deck were filled with white ambulances, each with a huge red cross painted on top.

The captain took me off the watch list—for awhile, at least—in order for me to spend more time on navigation. The man who took my place on the watch list was Ensign Bob Crites of Indianapolis, Ind. He was a second new officer and had arrived about a week earlier. He and six men came aboard when we exchanged one of our LCVPs for an LCS (landing craft support). We now had four LCVPs, having been ordered to give one to another LST.

We still had all six boat crews, so this was a net gain in personnel of one officer and six men. Bob had taken part in the invasions of Kwajalein, Eniwetok, and Saipan. He and his boat crew came from Pearl Harbor aboard another LST and had been with them until now. He regretted that the days were gone when he could go back and rest up in Honolulu after each invasion.

One of our seamen, Bill McGuire of North Braddock, Pa., became very ill with appendicitis, and we were fortunate this time to have capable medical personnel aboard to take care of him. The surgery was conducted in 45 minutes, under amazingly favorable conditions. McGuire came through in fine shape and soon was resting easily.

Our wardroom was equipped for such operations, with a large floodlight directly over one of the tables. Other lights were set to go on automatically in case of power failure. The other tables were used for laying out dressings and equipment.

The surgeon who performed the operation was Captain P. A. Koestner, U. S. Army (M.C.). The other doctors took over as nurses and attendants. McGuire got the operation for the same cost as an APC capsule.

Quite by chance I met Dr. John L. Savage of Winnetka, Ill., a couple of years ago. During the war he was Major Savage, Division Surgeon of the 33rd (Illinois) Infantry Division, and it was our *LST 698* which carried him and the 108th Medical Battalion from Finschhafen to Morotai. He recalled well the appendectomy and remarked that Captain Koestner was one of their most experienced surgeons.

We felt this was quite an event, but it didn't match the many-times-told tale of the pharmacist's mate in the submarine who performed the surgery with a penknife!

We had all been getting more shots recently. I had had my first typhus shot a couple of weeks earlier, followed by shots for cholera and plague. Then my second typhus shot. We were to have one more shot of each of the three.

I had been reading Victor Heiser's *American Doctor's Odyssey.* Much of the locale was the Philippine Islands. With such diseases as cholera and plague prevalent in this part of the world, it was good to know that the Army and Navy paid so much attention to preventive medicine.

Another thing that impressed me in Heiser's book was the amount of disease they had on shipboard, compared with us. We had had almost no sickness at all. In the Pacific, with so much sunshine and warm weather, it must have been one of the healthiest places we could be. I hadn't seen any sign of a cold so far. Also, we had a clean ship and had so far been fortunate never to have had a rat aboard.

On Sunday we had a Christmas service in the bow, on the truck ramp. It was conducted by an Army chaplain, one of our passengers. It was still hard to believe Christmas was almost upon us, but the Christmas carols were good to hear. Two were sung by a sextet (our quartet augmented by two Army men).

The chaplain, a Methodist, conducted a Catholic rosary service in the middle of the week. (He wasn't able to act officially when they operated on McGuire, who is Catholic—but he visited him regularly as a friend.)

We had a quiz program and spelldown, chiefly for the Army but with a number of Navy men participating. They asked me to be one of the judges, which meant tallying the scores.

Dr. Koestner, who operated on McGuire, timed the contestants by giving them two heartbeats, after which he gave them the gong by hitting his knife against an empty 40mm shell. The chaplain arranged the program, and another doctor acted as quizmaster. Prizes were bars of candy, with booby prizes of bars of Lifebuoy soap.

19

On Morotai, a *Tropical* Christmas

We beach on Morotai and unload our passengers and vehicles. Just in time, we receive Christmas mail, inczluding smashed fruitcakes. High-altitude nuisance air raids. Radio brings us Christmas music

December 1944—When we reached Morotai on 17 December, we discovered a pleasant little island. It lay in the cradle of Halmahera, east of Borneo and the Celebes in what was then the Netherlands East Indies. Specifically, Morotai was one of the Moluccas, formerly the Spice Islands.

The island was about 2 degrees north of the equator—as tropical as they came, with coconut palms and banana trees. Interesting-looking hills were visible in the distance.

Our ships arrived at daybreak, and one by one our LSTs beached side by side, in a long line. The minute we rolled up onto the beach, we were met by bulldozers, which scooped a road up to our bow ramp. A few moments later the vehicles were rolling off, first from the tank deck and then down a truck ramp from the main deck. The LSTs proved once more that where there were no docks, they were *the* answer.

Our crew found out from the medics that there was a nurses' compound nearby. Suddenly some of the men were volunteering for watch duty in port—knowing they'd then have use of binoculars.

Later we anchored in a calm harbor, surrounded by a few small islands, with a sandy beach and lots of coconut palms. From the harbor we could see the peaks of Halmahera in the distance. Smoke was rising from a volcano 50 or 60 miles away.

MacArthur's units had invaded Morotai on 15 September. By the time we got there, the Army had taken over enough of the island for its purposes. Despite our having the base only a short time, the roads were blacktopped. The engineers had established a sawmill.

Each base had a purpose, and the engineers came in to build roads, put up buildings, lay airstrips, and get everything functioning.

The mail we had all been waiting for came just before Christmas when Bark and one of our LCVPs came alongside with five big sacks of mail. It would make a different day for the men on *LST 698*.

It certainly did something for *me*. I got 15 letters from Fran, nine from others, two copies of *Time* (30 October and 20 November). The 30 October issue told of the Leyte invasion. I had waited a long time for it.

I got a Christmas package from my brother Lyman. It had a big "fragile" sticker on it. I was glad it was well wrapped and not like some of the packages that came that day. Some were smashed. Gum drops, shaving cream, chewing gum, cigarettes, glasses of jelly, etc., were scattered all around the mail sack. Really a mess! Someone had mailed a liquid, which had run all over the inside of the mailbag and obliterated the addresses on many of the packages.

Returning from a trip to the base, I went down to the boat dock and hooked a ride back to our ship, using a harbor boat doing taxi service. A couple of PT officers aboard wanted to pick up three cans of paint from a liberty ship. The ship's crew carefully lowered the first can down to the boat with a heaving line, but then the PT officer got wise. "Go ahead, toss it down," he said. "I'll catch it."

The fellow on the ship took him up on it and tossed the second can down. Naturally the PT officer *didn't* catch it—it was too heavy. And when the can hit the boat, the lid flew off, and black paint scattered in every direction. I was some 10 feet away and fared better than most, but I got paint all up and down my pant legs. Paint flew over everything on the stern sheets of the boat. It was a mess. But no one got sore, including the coxswain whose boat had to be repainted.

On Christmas Eve the Army chaplain who came with us from Finschhafen returned to our ship in the afternoon to give us a special Christmas service (his fourth of the day). He brought along a quartet of Army singers who could really sing—and a portable GI organ. We held the service in the forward part of the tank deck, to get out of the hot sun. The open bow doors and ramp gave us a nice breeze.

In his sermon, the chaplain pointed out something I'd never thought of—a tropical Christmas. That was what the first Christmas was—not a Christmas of snow and ice but a Christmas under a semitropical sun, with coconut palms, camels, and date trees. The comparison made Christmas in the tropics a little less strange.

At Morotai we had an air raid nearly every night. Three red tracers shot into the air, and in an instant all our ships and base installations were completely blacked out. (At sunset we darkened ship except for anchor lights.) Earlier, some raids had done considerable damage to planes and runways. The Japanese sent over a plane or two at any hour of the night. They came in so high that they were out of sight—and out of the range of our guns. But the anti-aircraft units on the base could detect them a long way out and either repel them or keep them so high that they were ineffective. However, the chaplain said the men on shore had been building foxholes just in case.

On Christmas Eve a number of our men came up to officers' country to wish us a merry Christmas. Some seemed to be more jovial and rosy-faced than usual. It was evident that someone had been tampering with the pharmacist's mate's "medicinal alcohol."

When the G.Q. sounded, all hands ran to their battle stations, which for most of them were gun tubs. One look at that Japanese "Betty" in the searchlights and we heard one of the men shout out, I'll get that—(fill it in with anything you can think of, and you'll get it on the first try). He opened up with his 20mm. Right away Ray Kennedy, the gunnery officer, started hollering into the voice box, "Cease firing, cease firing!" By then two or three others had joined in, but within a few seconds, they stopped. As I had mentioned, this Betty was out of range even to the shore batteries, to say nothing of an LST's 20 and 40mm guns.

The captain, as often was the case when in port, was enjoying himself over on another ship. He wondered what crazy fool was firing.

He was a bit chagrined when he returned to learn the crazy fool was on his own ship.

(Dr. Savage told me of seeing that plane from the shore. In fact, he had watched as it *was* shot down by the shore batteries and splashed into the sea.)

Christmas Day was far different from any we ever had before—but it *was* a holiday, and the Christmas spirit prevailed. The radio seemed to bring it closer to us. The programs were wonderful all day. The "Jungle Network" gave us hour after hour of carols and hymns and special programs, transcribed earlier in the United States.

One thing tickled me. A variety program included a conversation with Cellist Gregor Piatigorski, Chico Marx and Dinah Shore. They were discussing presents they had received that morning. Well and good, except that with our time difference it was 5 o'clock Christmas morning back in New York!

(We were nine hours earlier than Greenwich and 14 hours earlier than Chicago. Our days were exactly 12 hours long. Sunrise and sunset fell at the convenient hours of 0630 and 1830. But further east within the time zone those times got earlier and earlier.)

We had a fine turkey dinner at noon, and our wardroom had white tablecloths and napkins, which were *really* something extra. Every man was given a carton of cigarettes and half a box (10 packages) of Life Savers. We also had dishes of hard candy on every table, for fellows to stuff themselves with all day.

I had received a box of snacks in the mail and tried to fix a tray of hors d'oeuvres for supper. The chief (Angelo Prezioso) helped by adding some tuna fish to the anchovies and chicken pâté. He also scattered ripe olives around. I saved some of the food for another day.

Three days later more mail arrived, and 25 or 30 more fellows got their Christmas boxes from home.

20

Frantic Search for a 1945 Almanac

The handy Rolow paints the hull below the water line. A
6th Army engineering unit comes aboard. Problems getting
off the beach. We have no 1945 almanac! On New Year's
Day we set off for Lingayen Gulf, Luzon

January 1945—We started the new year with a bright-looking, freshly painted ship. The painting had begun about a month earlier. Then we got underway on short notice and weren't able to go ahead with the job. But in Morotai we had plenty of time to get it done.

Before Christmas the men scraped off the rust and applied a special anti-corrosive paint. Now for two days Willard Rolow, our motor machinist from Turner, Ore., had been busy with the spray gun, painting the hull black, dark green, and light green in standard camouflage pattern.

He painted the starboard side on one day. Then the ship's list was changed from port to starboard so that he could paint the port side. The reason for giving the ship a list was to reach down a little below the waterline. Of course, when the ship was empty, it stood considerably higher in the water.

Rolow worked part of the time from a raft in the water and sometimes from an LCVP with a ladder in the bow. Bill Eklund worked with him in the boat, sometimes taking a run out to see how it looked.

If you were to see Rolow, you would likely get a strange first impression. He always seemed to be covered with grease and grime—and the last two days, paint. He was one of the chief's motormacs. He could run any piece of equipment, repair any piece of machinery, and seemed to be able to do anything.

As with Stubby Green, I couldn't see how the other ships could function without him. If we wanted someone to run a forklift, we got Rolow. To operate the crane on the main deck, we got Rolow. To climb the mast and fix the ship's whistle, we got Rolow. If someone's watch didn't run, Rolow fixed it for him. One day when the baker was sick, Rolow baked the day's supply of bread. He was one of those guys who was gifted in anything mechanical—or otherwise.

My .45 got its first workout while we were at anchor in Morotai. There was some commotion on the deck while I was deck officer. The men had cornered a rat—the first and only one to come aboard our ship. The rat ran into a long tube which was not attached to anything, so they lifted the tube and shook the rat into the water.

Just then our skipper came alongside in one of the LCVPs and yelled to me: "Hand me your .45!" I did and from about 10 feet he fired seven rounds. On the seventh he got him.

With the year nearly at an end, the captain and I had been keenly aware that we had received neither an air almanac nor a nautical almanac for 1945. One or the other was essential in celestial navigation for working out star sights to determine our ship's position. So I went back to hitchhiking. I caught one ride after another and saw a good share of the base, trying to track down an almanac. But no luck. Undoubtedly ours were in the mail, but these wouldn't do us much good if they came after we sailed.

We pulled up anchor and sailed to the east side of Morotai where we beached the ship, running full speed in order to pull the bow up on the sand as far as possible. We dropped the stern anchor a short distance out in order to hold the ship perpendicular to the beach and then filled the forward ballast tanks to maintain our position.

As soon as a road was built up from the shore to our bow ramp (and those of other LSTs alongside us), we commenced loading a 6th Army engineering unit, including eight officers, 185 men, bulldozers, graders, and everything they needed to build roads from Lingayen to Manila. This included Bailey bridges designed to be quickly erected over rivers and streams where bridges had been wiped out or were inadequate.

When loading was completed, the ships were supposed to pull off one at a time and return to anchorages in the harbor. Only one problem: None of the nine or ten ships could pull off. They ran their engines full speed in reverse, took a strain on the stern anchor, and absolutely nothing happened.

Soon they started a maneuver in unison to try to free us up. On directions from the guide ship, the ships hoisted a flag to port and ran their port engines full speed, taking a strain on the stern anchor. Then they reversed it, running starboard engines.

Once, when the captain's order from the conn was, "Take a strain on the stern anchor," the reply came back, "The stern anchor is housed, Sir."

"What?" The skipper was furious. "Have the first lieutenant report to the conn." Bill Eklund came running up the ladder to explain that on the last maneuver the anchor had broken ground and they ended up hauling it all the way in. "Next time let me know when something like that happens," he screamed, trying to regain composure.

Finally, after about an hour, one ship managed to break loose and backed out into the bay. This ship then passed a cable to each of the others in turn until they were all afloat once more. We then returned to the anchorages for refueling.

Later, after I had just had a shower and tucked myself into bed, the special sea detail sounded, and I had to run up to the conn to navigate for a shift of anchorages. We had been alongside another LST, giving them part of the oil we received from a tanker that afternoon. I had expected that we'd stay tied up all night. Lighted buoys were nonexistent. But there was a full moon, so we had no trouble and we got the ship safely anchored.

No one paid much attention to New Year's Eve. It didn't have as much meaning as Christmas Eve. Ralph and I were both writing letters. Miller came in with his little idea, in case we were stuck for something to say. His suggestion: "Well, I'll write you again next year."

In my letter to Fran, I was expressing my concern about our new arrival, due on approximately Fran's birthday in February. "I presume I'll be able to write you again in ample time before your birthday and our little one's 'birth day.' But I don't know how long we'll be away from a post office. I've never felt more helpless in my life, with such an exciting event about to take place in our family and yet not be able to even hold your hand.

"I know this will be a happier year for us. We're just that much closer to being back together again. And this will be the first year for all *three* of us to be together."

We still had not located an almanac. So I spent most of the morning of New Year's Day on the island, bouncing around from base to base in one jeep after another. I succeeded only in obtaining a stock of writing paper from the Red Cross, a dozen pencils from the Army, and a dozen from the Navy. These had been scarce items.

However, the Captain of the Port, who had one almanac, mimeographed certain columns for January, so that we'd not be caught short. Most of the ships here, apparently, were in the same fix—a consequence of extended supply routes. This, too, never was discussed in midshipman school at Northwestern!

When I got back, I was really dirty. Some of these jeeps didn't have windshields, and the dust piled on me in layers. It was easy to get a ride in a jeep. The first fellow who had room picked you up. But we had found that he might just be going up to another camp a quarter mile down the road.

I had been walking about half a mile from one road to the next, and I saw a cow, big as life, in among the banana trees. This was the first cow I had seen since we left Oahu. I had scarcely seen any natives here. After visiting a naval base quite a distance off, I had asked how far we were from the perimeter. "Oh, it's about a mile up there," he said casually.

When the skipper returned, *he* had obtained an almanac. Just in time, before we sailed!

We had a fine New Year's dinner. Turkey again, with all the sliced white meat we could eat. Mince pie for dessert. Afterwards I saw a soldier walking across the deck with big pieces of turkey in each hand, which he had picked up in the galley. I guess that getting "seconds" on something like turkey was a real treat, and he was making the most of it.

That New Year's afternoon we hauled up the anchor and got underway with our convoy for Lingayen Gulf, on the island of Luzon in the Philippines, for our second invasion. Again our OTC (officer in technical command) was in *LST 917.*

21

Bridge-Builders Invade Luzon

For four days we sail through beautiful Philippine waters
from Leyte Gulf to Lingayen Gulf. We unloaded vehicles
and equipment onto a pontoon bridge from our bow doors to
the shallow shore

January 1945—The next big step in winning the Pacific war was the amphibious assault on Lingayen Gulf. On the west side of Luzon in the Philippines, roughly 100 miles north of Manila, this was prize territory for the Japanese. It would be defended vigorously.

But first it had been necessary to protect our position in Leyte. Heavy rains and unanticipated swamp conditions had made airport construction much slower than expected, preventing full use of our aircraft. And Japanese troops had been pouring into Leyte from the west. Consequently, on 5 December American amphibious forces had made landings at Ormoc, on Leyte's west coast. Ten days later, to open a safe seaway to Luzon, our troops had landed on Mindoro, an island on the western side of the Philippines, just south of Luzon.

The ships involved in those landings were suddenly challenged by Japanese planes and a scary new threat—"kamikaze" suicide planes. Five LSTs and five Liberty ships were sunk at Mindoro.[1] With these changing circumstances, the date for the Lingayen landings was rescheduled from 20 December to 9 January.[2]

"Troops for the Lingayen landing were lifted from 16 different bases in the South and Southwest Pacific, all but one of which—Nouméa—the Allies had wrested from the Japanese," according to Samuel Eliot Morison.[3] Our LST 698 was part of Task Group 77.9 Reinforcement Group under Rear Admiral Conolly, and we were scheduled to arrive at Lingayen Gulf on 11 January (A-day plus 2).

En route we rendezvoused with a huge convoy of ships which appeared on the horizon to the east and north of us—LST Flotilla 3, some 50 LSTs with destroyer escorts, and PCs (patrol craft) as screen. The ships came from such points as Bougainville, Oro Bay, Hollandia, Noemfoor, and Sansapor. Again we were under Commander A. A. Ageton, "best known as an authority on celestial navigation."[4] Our LSTs from Morotai merged into the convoy, and we took positions indicated in our invasion plan. We continued with the flotilla toward the Philippines.

Our guests, the Army engineers, would be responsible for building roads and erecting bridges on Luzon to speed the advance of troops to Manila. The after end of our tank deck carried Bailey bridges that could be assembled like an Erector set over rivers in advance of the troops.

A heavy pounding suddenly interrupted our quiet, peaceful cruise, as if all our 20-millimeter guns were going off at once. I was in the charthouse at the time. We found that Rolow was right outside on our navigation bridge, using an air hammer he had borrowed from the Army to chip away rust and paint. The amazing Rolow came through with another stunt to add to his list of accomplishments—paint chipping on a grand scale.

Gilbert and Sullivan would have you believe that the prime occupations of sailors were swabbing decks and polishing brass. But on a fighting ship, the big problem was keeping the rust off the steel deck. This required hour after hour of tough work, down on hands and knees, hammering and scraping the paint and rust. After that the deck was painted with a bright yellow coating of zinc chromate paint, the wartime substitute for orange or red lead paint we had always seen on steelwork. This was then covered with black deck paint.

Rolow was hammering away for all he was worth, rust and paint flying all over. What a racket!

Everyone was for stopping him (except for the fellows who had to do the chipping by hand), but no one had a good reason to stop such industry. Finally Monty, who was just below where Rolow had been working, came running up to the bridge, "It's knocking out the lights below," he said.

That was enough. They finally got Rolow to quit. You'd have to go a long way to find someone who'd *volunteer* to run one of those electric hammers. But that's Rolow for you.

Eventually we came to the entrance to Leyte Gulf, between Dinagat and Homonhon islands, where we had passed in October on our way to the Leyte landings. But this time we bore left into the Surigao Strait and southwest through the Mindanao Sea, passing Leyte, Panaon and Bohol on the north and Mindanao on the south. This was the start of about four days of sailing through Philippine waters. The voyage carried us into the Sulu Sea, passing Negros, Panay, and Mindoro on our right. Eventually we sailed into the South China Sea and north along the west coast of Luzon.

The Bombardment and Fire Support Group, which had proceeded three days ahead of the first amphibious forces, had been under attack almost from the moment they left Leyte Gulf. The slow-moving minesweeping and hydrographic group had received the first blows on 3 January when a suicide plane had crashed onto the deck of an oiler, killing two men but doing little damage to the ship.

The Allied Forces were soon aware that the kamikaze planes were back. The aircraft plants in Japan had continued to turn out planes, and though aviators were harder to replace, the Kamikaze Corps gave the Japanese an opportunity to provide quantities of low-cost planes for suicide missions, using pilots who possessed "more guts than training."[5]

The Japanese threw everything they had against the Allied forces during that first week of January. They sank two ships and damaged 25 in the first four days (3 through 6 January). One ship, the heavy cruiser *Australia,* was hit by five suicide planes in four days.[6]

The cruiser *Boise,* carrying General MacArthur to the Lingayen landings, once maneuvered to avoid torpedoes from a midget submarine. Two days later a bomb splashed into the water on its quarter, and on the same day the cruiser drove off another attacking plane.[7]

Philippine Travels

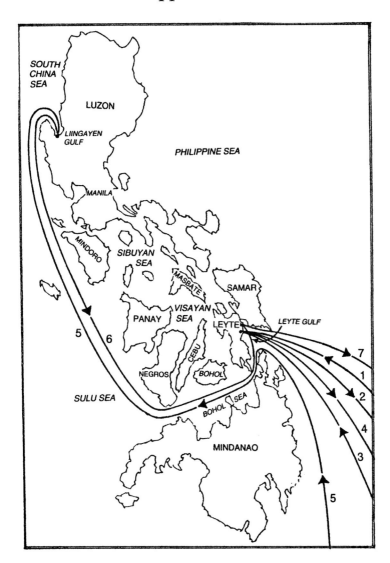

Our visit to the Philippines took us: 1) from Manus to Leyte, 2) to Hollandia, 3) Biak to Leyte, 4) to Hollandia, 5) Morotai to Lingayen Gulf, Luzon, 6) Lingayen Gulf to Tacloban, Leyte, 7) to Manus.

Between 3 and 13 January 1945, 46 American and Allied ships were hit or in a near miss by kamikazes, resulting in 738 men killed or missing and 1,377 wounded.[8]

But the Japanese were limited by the number of planes and pilots they could muster, and by the time our reinforcement group came along, the skies were quiet.

This turned out to be one of our most interesting cruises, because much of the time we were within sight of land. The water was calm compared with the open sea of a couple of days before. Once we saw a large white house with a red roof that looked like a large estate but could very well have been a hospital.

At one point we passed a very strange "convoy" on its way to Lingayen. An amazing variety of small craft, barges, tugs with tows, etc. All it needed was a sailboat with red sails. This was one of the few convoys that our flotilla of LSTs steaming at nine knots could possibly overtake. It illustrated the organization necessary to win a war. How long would it take for these little fellows to get to Lingayen?

Although we were usually in sight of land, it was often too far away to be a reliable navigation tool. I needed to shoot the stars and sun. The combination of celestial navigation and piloting gave me an extra workout. We also ran into stiff currents, which added to the complications.

As we passed Luzon, sailing through the China Sea, we stayed about 100 miles off the coast.

We heard about the 9 January landings on Lingayen in a broadcast of the Philippine Hour, but not until 10 January. We didn't hear a word of it the day before, although many were hanging around the loudspeaker. I guessed we wouldn't hear the whole story till we read about it in *Time*. But it seemed to be another great step towards ending the war. I wrote to Fran:

"It's hard to imagine what it was like over here a year ago, when the Japanese still had most of New Guinea, Guam and Saipan and even the Marshalls, when all our supplies to the southwest Pacific had to go the long route down to Australia and back up. Hawaii, then a frontier, was now as safe as Wisconsin. In another year what would this place be like?"

On 11 January my day began at 0200, when I got up to navigate as we approached the harbor. So by 1030 in the morning I had put in a pretty good eight-hour day. I made up for it after dinner at noon, when I slept for a good two hours.

Lingayen Gulf was a large, open bay, and our LST rolled just as much at anchor in the bay as it might on the high seas. It was seldom that the ship rolled at sea, and practically never in port. We had general quarters when a bunch of ack-ack from machine guns started down the bay. One of our signalmen reported seeing a Japanese Zero aircraft.

We found we were just sitting around the harbor, waiting for our turn to move up to the beach to unload. The delay was caused by the extremely shallow beach, requiring the ships to unload vehicles onto causeways. We had brought two sections, each about 250 feet long, with us, fastened to cleats that had been welded to our port and starboard bulkheads. At the destination these causeway sections had been released and towed by LCVPs to form causeways to the shore.

For five days we sat at anchor, waiting to unload. Fortunately the Army officers were amiable folks, just biding their time along with us. One of their officers, a dentist whom we called Doc, had brought along a bunch of phonograph records, and we were able to get an Ink Spots record from him in a swap. Doc was well-established as a raconteur. He was dramatic. And he'd tell a story in a way that made us laugh. When he didn't have a story, he'd keep on talking anyway—all evening.

He had brought an amazing assortment of things with him. One night he decided to have a feast. So he produced tuna fish, sardines, Spam, canned lobsters, deviled ham, and fruitcake, which everyone proceeded to devour while he told some of his funniest stories.

At last, on the afternoon of 16 January, we beached at a causeway on Yellow-Crimson Beach.

Shortly after we beached, an empty LST retracted from the beach on our starboard side, and another LST took its place. It came in too close, and its protruding cleats scraped against our starboard side. By evening the heavy surf on the beach caused that LST, with its exposed cleats, to continually hit against our bulkhead about two feet above the water line. One bulkhead began to give way, and other bulkheads to a lesser degree. Just before midnight seams along the starboard side opened and the ship began to take water slowly. The crew immediately installed shoring. That morning, bulldozers and graders began to run off the ship over the causeway.

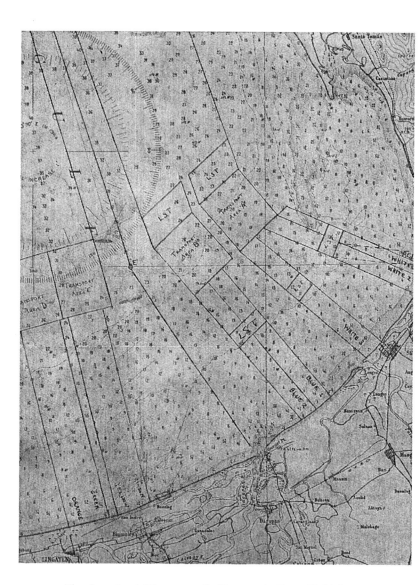

The beach at Lingayen Gulf was shallow. Vehicles
traveled from the LSTs to the beach over causeways
that had been carried in 250-foot lengths by the LSTs
(hung from cleats welded to the bulkheads). *U.S. C. &
G. S. 4209.*

We saw about 100 Filipinos on the beach—men, women, and children. The men were often in skivvy shirts, shorts, and straw hats. The women wore attractive dresses but were barefoot. Youngsters ran around everywhere. Trading was not yet the fine art it had become in Leyte, where the Americans had been for a longer time.

By 1115 the vehicles and supplies, Army officers and 185 men had disembarked. We pulled back from the causeway and returned to an anchorage in the harbor. The shoring of our starboard bulkhead seemed to be holding.

We were well aware that not everybody had fared so well as we. And much was happening that we didn't know anything about at that time. For example, the planes of Task Force 38 had assisted our landings by hitting the airfields of Luzon and Taiwan, destroying many of the Japanese planes. There still had been plenty of kamikazes left to attack the earlier ships. But our reinforcement group, arriving at Lingayen Gulf on 11 January, had an easier job than the earlier ships in delivering its troops and cargo to Luzon. It owed much to Task Force 38 and to all the ships that preceded our LST through the Philippine waters.

On 18 January we got underway, forming into a convoy to return to Leyte.

Notes

[1]   Morison, Samuel Eliot: *The Two-Ocean War,* Little, Brown and Company, New York, 1972, 403

[2]   Barbey, Daniel E.: *MacArthur's Amphibious Navy,* Naval Institute Press, Annapolis, 1969, 279

[3]   Morison, Samuel Eliot: *History of the United States Naval Operations in World War II, Volume XIII, The Liberation of the Philippines; Luzon, Mindanao, the Visayas, 1944-1945,* Little, Brown and Company, New York, 1959, 97

[4]   *Ibid., 144*

[5]   *Ibid., 99*

[6]   *Ibid., 325-26*

[7]   *Ibid., 115-16*

[8]   *Ibid., 325-26*

22

A Vital Lesson in Navigation

Returning from Lingayen, our 0800 radar fix differs greatly from the positions of any of the other ships in the convoy. Who was right? Was a catastrophe averted?

(The following is from a letter written over 35 years ago (18 June 1967) by Ed Erickson, supply officer on our *LST 698: "Homer, did you ever tell those kids of yours about how you saved the convoy in the China Sea on the way back from Lingayen? If you didn't, I'm reminding you you should."*)

January 1945—Something happened on 20 January that might not happen again in years. Cruising through Philippine waters on our return from the invasion of Lingayen Gulf, the convoy guide got off on his navigation but didn't know it. So did most of the other ships. It remained for our ship, the *LST 698*, to change the course of the whole convoy.

After an invasion, a convoy was formed each day to include all ships which had completed their assignments. This could be quite a motley group, since their common denominator was that they had unloaded and were ready to go. Our convoy from Lingayen Gulf on this day was indeed a motley group. It consisted of 18 LSTs plus one under tow, two APDs (high-speed transports—converted destroyers) under tow, 20 LCIs (landing craft infantry), and a screen of four destroyers and six PCs (patrol craft). We were designated as Task Unit 78.11.8, with OTC in *LST 701*.[1]

On 18 January, the convoy got under way about sunset, as was customary, so that it could start out under a cover of darkness. Our destination was Tacloban, on San Pedro Bay at the north end of Leyte Gulf. We were to follow essentially the same course through the Philippines that we had taken to Lingayen Gulf, but in reverse.

Once we got under way, I was taken off the watch list again, so that I could concentrate on navigation. Some ships undoubtedly got by with minimum navigation, just enough to obtain 0800, 1200 and 2000 positions for the log, relying on the convoy guide to get the ships to their destination and away from shoals. But Captain Gilbert took a particular interest in good navigation. As a "mustang" (former enlisted man), he had once been a chief quartermaster and assistant navigator on a destroyer.

Our executive officer, Ken Saunders (Sandy), was officially the ship's navigator, as previously mentioned. But he was sick, and so with the captain's occasional review, I had been doing all the navigation on this trip.

As we left Lingayen Gulf, the ship had been rocking and shaking, because we were heading into a trough. When we turned to start our southward journey through the China Sea, it began to roll instead of shake. On the first day out, the sea calmed down. But it became very cloudy, so no stars were visible that evening.

Early in the morning of 20 January the convoy changed its course to the southeast in order to approach Mindoro Strait, west of the island of Mindoro. It was still so overcast that we had no chance to obtain a position from the stars. And we were out of sight of land, ruling out obtaining our position by piloting—using landmarks or man-made navigation aids.

But there was radar. This was something new in World War II. It wasn't because of eating carrots that our anti-aircraft squads could spot enemy aircraft at such a distance. It was radar.

We had one simple radar unit on our LST. Its four-mile scope was useful in maintaining our position in a convoy, because it gave accurate readings of the distance to the ship ahead and could readily detect a change in that distance. The 20-mile scope was used in bringing a ship into or out of a harbor, supplementing piloting when visibility was limited. The 80-mile scope could pick up ships or land at a much greater distance, but it was rarely used for navigation.

"Tex" Bavousett, of Fort Worth, Texas, our principal radarman, was a rosy-faced, curly-haired teenager who was always curious about the potential of the machine he was entrusted with. He might ask, "Is there a school of fish off the port bow?" He had spotted them on the tube.

The Philippine waters were an ideal location to experiment with radar navigation. We were often out of sight of land, but the radar provided very accurate readings of nearby mountain peaks or sharp high points on land. This gave us both the peak's relative bearing (the angle between the ship's direction and the object) and its distance from the ship. The *edges* of islands could *not* be used, because of the way they tapered off into the sea.

A single observation could produce a navigational fix, provided that the readings were precise, the navigation chart was accurate, and the peak or other point of observation was properly identified. But we always checked its accuracy by making a second observation, using a different peak. The readings of the second object should produce a fix in exactly the same location as the first. A third sight with the same result could make you even more certain.

Through the night we had been sailing southbound on a course of 174 degrees and at 0703 we had changed our heading to the southeast, 146 degrees. Tex and I went to the radar and found some promising peaks on Mindoro, some 50 or 60 miles to the east. We checked them out, and it worked.

The fix obtained from this radar position, using two peaks, put us far south of our dead-reckoning track (the line we had made on the navigation chart to indicate our advance since our last fix). But we felt quite confident about our position. It revealed that we had been set ahead by currents during the night, a common occurrence in the Philippines. The currents had pushed us 17 miles south of our dead-reckoning track position. With the course change to the southeast, it appeared that we were now traveling on a course 17 miles south of our previous dead reckoning track (and parallel to it).

It was a navy requirement for each ship in a convoy to post its position at 0800 by raising a flag hoist showing its current latitude and longitude. In this way ships can check their positions with the others in the convoy. The captain looked carefully at our radar position and told the signalmen to post it.

The other ships posted their positions, too, but none had our position, and most were pretty close to the dead reckoning track we had advanced through the night. With the wide divergence between our position and those of the other ships, the captain had stuck his neck out a mile—or 17 miles!

After two hours the skipper began to get concerned about our posted position. He didn't want to get razzed by his fellow skippers in the convoy. So he asked us to review our position. It checked out perfectly with the previous one, advanced for the ship's travel along our new dead-reckoning track. With that information the skipper got off a message on the light to the guide ship something like this: "Our navigation indicates that our present course leads toward Merope Rock. How does this compare with your position?"

The reply: "You are 15 miles south of us and the destroyer and 12 miles south of the average of the ships [0800 positions]. Am checking but think we are on." We continued to check *our* position and continued to be convinced we were headed for shoal waters.

At 1024, according to our ship's log, the convoy changed course to the left from 146 degrees to 115 degrees. At 1242 we changed to 075 degrees. Then at 1312 we saw flags go up for another course change. It was *"two turn,"* an emergency maneuver that was executed immediately. All ships turned over the rudder instantly, and suddenly they were all traveling cattywampus, rather than in orderly columns, on a course of 055 degrees.

At that point we saw those rocks sticking out of the sea, about seven miles off our starboard beam. The ship's log reported our sighting the Apo Island lighthouse (nine and one-half miles east of the rock) at 1400, with a true bearing of 129 degrees, distance 15.5 miles. At 1403 the convoy changed the base course back to 075 degrees, returning the ships to columns after maneuvering to avoid the rock. It took two more course changes, at 1526 and 1638, to put us on a southward heading once more to traverse the Apo East Pass.

A message came on the signal light, from the guide ship to *LST 698*, "Looks like everyone was out of step but you."

At times the fellows had razzed me, saying: "What the hell—we just follow the ship ahead, anyhow." Probably so. But this time our efforts paid off. It made Tex and me feel good.

Actually, this episode did more to discredit other navigators, who had not worked out a radar position, than it did to praise the *698*. It was amusing (or perhaps alarming) to be right when the others were wrong, and it was a thrill when the ships changed course to avoid danger.

Naturally this made the skipper feel mighty good. And as I look back, it seemed as if I could do no wrong for the rest of our Pacific odyssey.

*   *   *

Recently I've obtained copies of the logs for the period for both our *LST 698* and the guide ship, *LST 701*, showing these positions for 20 January. (A minute of latitude equals one nautical mile—2,040 yards.)

	LST 698		*LST 701* (guide ship)	
HOUR	LATITUDE	LONGITUDE	LATITUDE	LONGITUDE
0800	13° 11'N	119° 36'E	13° 28'N	119° 36'E
1200	12° 48'N	119° 59'E	13° 00'N	120° 19'E
2000	12° 23'N	120° 50'E	12° 22'N	120° 49'E

Note that at 0800 *LST 701's* position was 17 miles north of ours. The 701's deck log remarks sheet for 20 January records the six course changes from 1024 to 1526 but contains no explanation.

After that we felt quite confident about using radar for navigation.

Notes

¹   War Diary, Commander LST Flotilla 6, 5-6

23

Tacloban, a Different Kind of Base

Built around existing city streets and buildings,
Tacloban uses old warehouses and stores for army and navy
supply depots, post office, private stores, and offices. Mud
and mail for everyone

January 1945—The remainder of our return cruise from Lingayen was quiet, with only one small crisis.

On our last evening I got up in the middle of the night for about three hours, to work in the chart house. We had been cruising roughly northeast through the Bohol Sea towards the Surigao Strait. As we approached the tight portion of the strait between the tip of Leyte and the northernmost point of Mindanao, the guide ship turned north a bit too soon, then zigged and zagged until they figured they could get the whole convoy through the opening. Altogether, according to the log, we changed course seven times in two and one-half hours.

Looking back now, more than 60 years later, I can imagine this was the first time that the guide LST, its skipper and its navigator had been responsible for leading a convoy. *LST 701* was commissioned later than the *698*, and its first invasion was at Lingayen Gulf.

By noon on 23 January, we had reached San Pedro Bay, an inlet at the top of Leyte Gulf between the islands of Leyte and Samar. The base, in the town of Tacloban, was different from any we had run into. It utilized city streets and buildings for its various units. Old stores and warehouses housed the various Army and Navy supply depots, post offices, shore patrol headquarters, etc. These activities were dumped into the original framework of the town. The natives still had their small shops, lawyers' offices, and residential districts.

Mud was everywhere. You could not avoid it. The streets were ankle-deep in it. The occasional sidewalks ran only where convenient. I went in to town with Bill Chapman, Al Toll and Bark, the mailman, to see about mail. On the way in, our boat went through rain, and it rained most of the day. So the mud was at its worst. I wore my high-top, rough-skinned G. I. shoes, which until then had had very little hard treatment. But the minute I stepped off the dock, the shoes were initiated. MacArthur waded up to his knees, so why shouldn't I wade up to my ankle tops?

We just plowed through the mud to the post office—and spent the rest of the afternoon there. We got current mail one place and were told to go down the street for our bag mail. We did, and discovered that LSTs in the 600 group had their mail in six piles 20 feet long, six feet high. We started digging and found sacks for *698* here, here, here, here, one place and another as we combed through the tags. Often we found a sack on the very bottom and had to pull out eight or ten sacks to get it out. We collected 26 sacks for the *698*, piled them up, then made arrangements for a truck to haul them over to the boat dock.

When we brought them back to the ship, you can imagine the commotion they aroused. We took them into the wardroom, and all the officers started sorting it out alphabetically. Soon mail call began. That was a happy evening for all aboard. Nearly everyone got 20 or 30 or 40 letters, plus many long-delayed Christmas presents! The *most* belated Christmas present was one sent to Bill Eklund—a nice little foot-high Christmas tree on a red stand with imitation snow on it—in plenty of time for St. Valentine's Day.

All at once I got 27 letters from Fran, plus letters from my dad, Fran's mother, my sisters, and various other relatives. Some of the fellows had received packages in shreds and tatters. We began to understand how futile it was to put "FRAGILE" stickers on the packages. Once the package got into a mail sack, no one ever saw the sticker.

The next day Bark came back from the Post Office with five more sacks of packages and two more of first-class mail, which included 14 more letters from Fran and a combination of Christmas and Valentine cards.

Half a century later Al Toll recalled in a letter to me: "When we were in the Philippines, Homer, you had a wistful, maybe worried look. I asked what was on your mind. You tried to be nonchalant but were concerned about mail from Fran. I guessed, 'Are you expecting a new arrival?' To which you rendered a broad smile."

One day I had the morning watch, then spent much of the afternoon observing the dealings at our fantail with natives in their outrigger canoes. Ever since we arrived, these native craft had been all over the harbor. We seemed to have two or three of them with us all the time. The natives had been weaving hats and little bags and purses of dubious value.

At first the standard unit of trade had been the skivvy shirt, but the market rapidly inflated, so that most items could not be had for less than a mattress cover or army blanket. They no longer even looked at skivvy shirts. However, the circulation of American victory money, in which the Army and natives had been paid, made them a little more free with their pesos and centavos in Japanese currency, of which there were fistfuls and fistfuls.

The natives and their canoes were quite a sight. Young people, both boys and girls, paddled around from ship to ship, striking bargains. They were pretty well dressed, the men in army clothes, the girls in plain cloth dresses. Most were barefoot and had been all their lives, as evidenced by the spread of their toes.

Al Toll and I wandered up a few streets of Tacloban. I got hold of some coins and American victory currency but found I could not send it through the mail. The coins were shiny and new, with a modern design. The 20 and 50 centavo coins were in wide circulation, but you had to see the natives to get the 5 or 10 centavo—the Army didn't bother with them.

The shops were the hole-in-the-wall type, open front, some selling hardware and a few staples, others dealing in a meager supply of souvenirs. There was a theater, not yet open but expected to open soon. The mud was not so bad as on our earlier trip. No longer up to my ankles. But it was impossible to walk through the town without getting mud an inch above the soles of the shoes.

Navy, Army, and natives were all mixed in together. I saw two old women with blouses and ill-fitting skirts carrying baskets on their heads. Girls of 12 and 14 ran around the town looking much more American than their parents. All but the old folks spoke pretty good English. The men and boys 16 and up (more or less) could get jobs at the employment center as laborers, carpenters, etc. The people were small, and Al Toll and I seemed to tower above them.

After an hour or two of sightseeing, Al and I went over to the officers' club on Samar, across the bay. There, under coconut trees, we drank a couple of bottles of Schlitz at picnic tables edged with green bamboo. An adjoining recreation center for the enlisted men was nearly finished—a pretty spot.

Our waiter, Sam, was a steward's mate third class in the Navy. He joined up in December and wore the olive drab fatigue uniform adopted by the Seabees. Sam said that when the Japanese were here, he was a guerrilla. We asked him how many Japanese he had shot. He smiled and said, "That I do not know, Sir. I just like to shoot." He was happy that the Americans were here. He said they treat them well and do not molest their women—although he said there were certain "business women" in the town. "When the Japanese were here," he said, "most of the natives went into the hills. Now, they're all back, beginning to lead normal lives again."

Time was up. We had to say good-bye to Tacloban and San Pedro Bay. Our LST joined a convoy bound for Manus, in the Admiralty Islands, which had been our final staging area for the invasion of Leyte last October. How much had happened in those past three months!

24

A Little Mail, Ten Tons of Meat

At Manus we receive much-needed fresh water, fuel oil,
boatloads of fresh provisions, charts, soap. Our bulkheads
are repaired in an advanced base sectional dock. More mail,
but not the letter I was looking for

February 1945—The water was blue and calm, and not a ripple in it as we sailed for Manus, in the Admiralties, in task group 79.5 with the OTC again in *LST 701.*

Once we were out of sight of land, it seemed as if we were moving very slowly. We wished we were going faster, because for the first time we had a fresh water shortage. Both evaporators, which together ordinarily produced enough fresh water for our daily consumption, conked out. We had been unable to take on additional water from a lighter for a month, and we were quite low. (We couldn't make our own fresh water while at anchor, because of the danger of pumping mud and sand into the evaporators.)

So we rationed fresh water, turning it on only for a half hour before meals. Salt-water showers. No laundry except in salt water, which left things stiff. (Toilets ordinarily used salt water anyway.)

We had a big clean-up day before we reached Manus. We aired mattresses and clothing, got clean sheets, and, to cap it all, turned the fresh water on for long enough for everyone to take a shower.

But we couldn't help thinking of the fellows on Leyte and Luzon who got covered in mud, and then, maybe in a couple of weeks, got a shower from a drizzling water bucket. Aboard ship, things were always reasonably clean. No dust. All we had to do was keep our pants away from greased cables and fresh paint. But we could still appreciate a shower!

All of us were looking forward to more mail, stocking up on fresh provisions, and eating real ice cream. No one had a greater interest in reaching port than I, awaiting possible news of a new son or daughter.

Once we reached our anchorage in Seeadler Bay, Manus, we dropped four boats into the water. One of course went to the base for mail. The results were sad. Two little packs of letters. But getting any mail at all was a good sign. At least the post office knew we were there. "If we've got it, you can have it."

I took most of our binoculars and navigational instruments over to the optical shop on a repair ship. Three fellows helped me carry the stuff. We were all loaded down. After we finished our business, we went through the ice cream line and got some for ourselves and the waiting boat crew. Ice cream was a big thing.

The next day was really busy. Eric (Ed Erickson), Ray Kennedy, Bill Chapman, the chief (Angelo Prezioso), and I went to the base with a big working party and two boats.

We began hauling supplies of all descriptions back to the ship. The most supplies, I guess, since we loaded up in New Orleans. Eric had submitted requisitions the day before, so most of the supplies were ready for us. We got a truck and quickly loaded it with such supplies as brooms, swabs, dust pans, baking trays, coffee cups, pencils, rope, pipe wrenches, Scotch tape. We just backed the truck up to the door of a big Quonset hut and loaded it on.

Next we got a load of soap and ship's service stores—cigarettes, candy, writing tablets, etc. I went back to the ship with this boatload and had chow. Imagine a whole boatload of soap and soap powder. We ought to be able to get the laundry done now, I thought. We had been practically out of both items.

Then Eric started on fresh provisions, with 20,000 pounds of meat! (No ration points needed.) This sounds like a lot and it was—it filled up practically all our freezer space—but we often carried as many as 200 extra passengers for weeks at a time. It was chiefly Australian and New Zealand beef and lamb—not so much variety as when we left the states, but it ought to fill the fellows up. Eventually the working party switched to dry provisions, canned foods, etc.

After dinner I went right back to the base and got some charts. This chart depot had nearly everything I wanted. When we had been here in October, we had to fight the whole fleet for stuff, but this time the harbor was relatively empty.

Next morning we got water, and we took everything they had. The ship was really thirsty. (Some of the older LSTs didn't have evaporators. I wondered how they managed.) We got diesel fuel in the afternoon. On Sunday we moored again to a water barge and took on more fresh water.

One afternoon when we had liberty, I went with some of the men as officer-in-charge. The fellows didn't care much about liberty here. They'd sooner get into a working party so that they could go over to the base. Those on liberty in Manus went to one of the little islands surrounding the harbor, to drink beer and go swimming. Each man was entitled to three beers. They drank it at "Duffy's Tavern," a large, open building with picnic benches on the sand. All this was quite an improvement over liberty when we were here before. Then, each ship had a slew of soldiers aboard, and the liberty island was so crowded that the men could scarcely sit down, say nothing of finding any shade. You can't imagine how little shade one coconut palm makes when the sun's directly overhead.

Now they had basketball courts, horseshoe pits, baseball fields, etc., but it was usually too hot to play. However, there was good swimming at the beach on the seaward side. Good sand. I wished I could go in, but I was on duty status. Once I got accidentally soaked when a surprisingly large wave rolled up about eight feet further than any before. It caught a bunch of us. Of course, I was dry in five minutes.

On 12 February we got another dribble of mail—a pack of December letters and a thin pack from Honolulu which brought us our February 5th copies of *Time*. One of the men at the post office said the mail was irregular, and the amount received recently had been very small. No telling when more might come in.

Next morning I went back to the base and collected our various binoculars and navigational instruments.

One day the Navy brought in a boatload of natives in an LCM and I watched them file past. All were dressed the same, with a large piece of cloth wrapped around them from their waists to their knees. That's all. The best dressed wore bright red. All were barefoot but walked easily on the sharp gravel. The Navy didn't have any women in this group—must have left them back in the hills. Where were the beautiful South Pacific maidens that you saw in the travel posters? (You know the posters: "Join the Navy—travel, adventure, experience, learn a trade.")

We learned that the island even had a Coca-Cola bottling plant. Bill Chapman, Ray Kennedy and Ralph Hart came back with 136 cases—enough to sell to the whole crew. Bill saw to it that they got it safely back to the storeroom and *locked up!*

On Sunday I worked for awhile in the chart house putting away some of the new charts and fixing my index.

At last, on 14 February, there was mail from home. I got wonderful letters from Fran for 3, 4, 5 and 8 February, and in the last letter I learned that she had one day to wait before she went to the hospital. She referred to her previous day's letter, which had not arrived. I judged she had seen the doctor and planned to induce labor on the 9th if the baby had not started on its own before then. On 16 February I got two more letters, for 25 and 27 January. As Monty (Bruce Montgomery of South Minneapolis, Minn.) said, "You still don't know whether you're a father or a mother."

On 17 February, two more letters came from Fran, for 6 and 7 February. Since I had already received her letter of the 8th, they added to my information but nothing new on her status.

We finally received a communication from the command that we were to proceed to the advanced base sectional dock for repairs to our starboard side, which had been damaged at Lingayen. The ABSD was a floating dry dock. It had been built in the United States and towed in sections across the Pacific to Manus, where it was assembled in Seeadler Harbor.

This ABSD—an Advanced Base Sectional Dock—is a floating drydock in Seeadler Harbor, Manus. Large enough to take a battleship, it holds here four 328-foot LSTs. Our *LST 698*, upper right, is repaired for bulkhead damage. *National Archives.*

It was huge—large enough to accommodate a battleship, but in this case four LSTs; two, side by side. The ships sailed into it at one end and moored to a side of the dock. Then the gates were closed and the water pumped out completely, leaving the ships supported on ways that fitted the contour of the ship's hull. The repair crews then swarmed into action to make the necessary repairs.

Fifty years later Al Toll recalled that almost all the officers and crew were involved in scraping barnacles. "We used long-handled scrapers, much like what we used to chop off icy streets. What a stinking, fishy-smelling job! I can see those barnacles now, throbbing. We smelled for a week afterward." Al also noted that the ABSD crew had quarters *under* the dry dock, not on the sides.

When repairs were completed on the four ships, water was pumped back in until the water level reached the level outside the dock. These docks were important innovations of World War II, where distances were so enormous. Often a single day in dry dock could put a ship back in service, avoiding many days or weeks of travel to another base.

Finally on 20 February we got underway, with still no word from Fran on the baby, or whether it was a boy or a girl. We were bound for Guadalcanal, where things had been hot in 1943 but a *long* way from the action in 1945.

25

Guadalcanal—and *It's a BOY!*

*We sail into the Solomons to Guadalcanal and Florida
Island, the scene two years earlier of some of the fiercest land
and sea fighting of the war. We find a baseball diamond, a
huge PX and a radio station. Finally, the mail that I was
looking for—a son born: William Ellis Haswell*

February 1945—Leaving Seeadler Bay, on the north side of
Manus in the Admiralty Islands, we sailed in Task Force 76 around
the east coast of the island, and headed south into the Bismarck Sea.
We passed between New Guinea and New Britain into the Solomon
Sea. Our destination was Port Purvis, Florida Island, located on
Ironbottom Sound across from Guadalcanal.

We had an odd navigational experience as we approached New
Guinea—an afternoon of island dodging. Well, not exactly that, but
confused navigation. These islands had never been sufficiently
explored and surveyed. The charts had little notes on them: 'This
island reported to be 2.1 miles, 195 degrees from charted position.
In other words, it was in the wrong place on the chart and could not
be used accurately to determine one's position. There were also
islands marked "E.D." (existence doubtful) and "P.A." (position
approximate).

It was a navigator's field day. I was on the conn all afternoon until supper. Sandy and I worked on it together.

We finally received word that we could say in our letters that we had been in the Lingayen Gulf invasion. I wrote to Fran that we had now been in two invasions and had scarcely seen the enemy. "An LST doesn't go looking for trouble. It moves slowly to its destination. When it's unloaded, it clears out. So a good share of the time it's behind the lines, a long way from the enemy. Not so for a destroyer or carrier. Thus an LST has its points. The 'Amphibs' are the joke of the regular Navy. They look ugly to an old seaman. Their chief virtue is their ability to run aground, which doesn't sound like a virtue to the regular Navy. And they're as informal as they come (which suits me just fine). But the Amphibs are doing a job out here, and as long as I've got to be here, it might as well be on an LST."

I was on regular watch duty this trip. One morning when I had the 8 to 12 watch it rained nearly all the time—*hard* rain. Despite foul-weather gear, I still felt wet enough to change to dry clothes when I came off watch.

We were the leaders this time and had squeezed enough knots to get in at dawn instead of noon. Naturally the sooner we got in, the sooner we'd be able to get our next mail. I had a particular interest in the matter, still waiting for word from Fran on whether we had a boy or girl. So did others. The captain had a $5 bet on its being a boy, and Lou Miller had $5 on a girl.

As we approached the Guadalcanal area, we had a good opportunity to check radar navigation against celestial. Sandy did the star sights, while Tex and I did the radar fix. The two came out within a pinpoint.

Closing in on Guadalcanal, I was busy tracking our course between islands. I had the 8 to 12 evening watch but spent much of the time in the chart room. Sandy relieved me about 2 and I turned in until I heard the special sea detail siren about 6.

We sailed into Ironbottom Sound. Guadalcanal was visible on the right, and little Savo Island on the left. Then we sailed somewhat northward, passing the small islands of Tulagi and Gavutu. When we came to Florida Island, we pulled into its bay, Port Purvis.

As related by Samuel Eliot Morison,

> That mountainous island [Guadalcanal] of the Solomons
> Group—only 90 miles long by 25 wide, inhabited by a few
> thousand woolly-haired Melanesians and offering no natural
> resources but mud, coconuts and malarial mosquitoes—was
> bitterly contested by the naval, air and ground forces of the
> United States and Japan for almost six months. In the Pacific
> war, Leyte and Okinawa may have been as stubbornly fought
> for as Guadalcanal; but this Solomon Island has had the
> distinction for being the scene of numerous pitched battles
> and the occasion of six major naval engagements within a
> space of four months. In addition there were half a hundred
> ship-to-ship and air-sea fights, only one of which in the
> superabundance of heavy slugging, attained the dignity of a
> battle name. Costly they were, too, both in ships and in men.
> You may search the seven seas in vain for an ocean graveyard
> with the bones of so many ships and sailors as that body of
> water between Guadalcanal, Savo and Florida Islands which
> our bluejackets named Ironbottom Sound.[1]

So now, two years later, we dropped anchor in a sleepy lagoon, surrounded by hills dense with jungle vegetation. Another wonderland of the tropics, with blue skies, white clouds and soft breezes drifting across the deck. At nightfall, we saw a sunset fit for a James Fitzpatrick travelogue, and then a tropical moon.

We were *still* waiting for mail. We felt the war was a wonderful developer of patience. It had been exciting to come into port, for the prospect of obtaining mail, but now we had to cool our heels for a couple of days or more.

I wrote, without disclosing our location, "We've added another port to our list. One by one we were visiting the places we had read about in the papers. Of course, it's different now, with volleyball courts and radio stations covering up the battle grounds of a few months ago. We're beginning to feel like old-timers ourselves. We saw a brand new LST, fresh from the States, with its LCT still perched on its main deck. Like old salts our men started telling newcomers about our invasions of Leyte and Lingayen, undoubtedly building them up into real sagas of the sea."

Next morning, following the 4 to 8 watch, I went over to the post office landing with Eric, Ralph, the chief, Bob Crites, Lou Miller, and a bunch of the men on various missions. I was surprised to find a grassy hillside with many kinds of trees. Picturesque thatched hut buildings instead of the usual bleak Quonset huts. Florida Island was really a pretty spot.

The Ironbottom Sound officers' club had the choicest location, up winding steps to the top of the hill, overlooking the picturesque bay made famous in the early part of the war by the number of ships that went to the bottom of it.

Part of the post office base was on one side of a point of land and part on the other, connected by a path over the hill. Along the path we saw all sorts of trees including a banana tree (no bananas), a papaya tree and others which, not being a botanist, I couldn't identify. My knowledge of tropical trees seemed limited to those which provided food.

Next day, still no mail. The captain fixed it up for me to go over to Guadalcanal and check with that post office where the mail is supposed to come before it is forwarded here. It would be a chance to see Guadalcanal.

I wrote on 28 February: "I had quite an interesting day, even if I wasn't able to do much more than satisfy my curiosity. I got up at 0530 and at 0600 was on the *LST 671*, which was making the trip to the larger island [Guadalcanal]. We messed around for quite a while, going to various ports on the island, so I didn't get ashore until about 1345—at a point about 20 miles from the fleet post office. I hitched a ride in a jeep with three Seabees, and we bounced over a gravel road, along the shore.

"We saw a number of sunken Japanese ships with their rusty bows stuck in the air and their names in both Japanese and English (one of them was the *Kyúsy Maru*, still plainly visible).

"We drove past a baseball field where men were playing in big-league uniforms. And we saw a couple of open-air theaters. Slightly

120

different from the average American's conception of this island. Marines and soldiers were fishing in streams. And jeeps and buses were running all over the place—on the right-hand side of the road for a change.

"As for the mail, I found out that the fleet post office had *LST 698* properly catalogued—in fact, had a complete history of our post office addresses since 2 June on a 3 x 5 card. And they said that our mail was being sent over to the other [Florida] island. There just must have been no mail coming in.

"After finding out about the mail, I walked to the recreation center, which consisted of a big Red Cross building with reading rooms and library, an Army PX and a canteen with lines formed to buy sandwiches, coffee, doughnuts, Cokes, popcorn, and ICE CREAM.

"I was amazed at the PX. It was the biggest I had seen since we left Pearl Harbor. It sold books, khakis and souvenirs in addition to the usual drug store items. I had to catch the ferry across to the other island, so I didn't take much time. I decided not to wait in the ice cream line. It was a block long. But I got a sandwich and doughnut.

"I hooked a ride in a jeep back to a dock where I caught an APC (auxiliary patrol craft) used as a ferry. I was talking to one of its officers at chow time and got myself invited to dinner (just in time to avoid a downpour) and had a pleasant time examining the ship. I got back to the post office landing just in time to catch a ride to our ship with the captain, who was finishing up at the officers' club."

It was 1 March when I finally learned that William Ellis Haswell had arrived at 10:06 p.m. *9 February* at Evanston Hospital. The news came all at once—Fran's letters from February 12th to 19th, her mother's, which she wrote on the 9th while waiting for Billy's arrival (completed when she heard the news), and letters of congratulations from Dad, Aunt Anna, my sisters Rachel and Helen, Fran's sister Helen Van, Bob Ela on leave in Madison, and even Wally Foster in West Virginia.

What a relief to hear at last—nearly three weeks after Billy was born! And here we were receiving congratulations from all these folks before his dad even knew whether he had a son or daughter.

It was not until I began to read Fran's account in depth that I learned how much she had gone through. She had waited until after the delivery to tell me how sick she had been beforehand.

I had the afternoon watch. So I found myself passing out cigars on the quarterdeck after passing them out in the wardroom.

Notes

[1]   Morison, Samuel Eliot: *History of U. S. Naval Operations in World War II, Volume V, The Struggle for Guadalcanal, August 1942-February1943,* Little, Brown and Company, New York, 1949, 3-4

26

A Radio That's Just for Listening

The radio shack's radios were mainly for communication with other ships. A new radio was wired to reach all the living areas of the ship with music and entertainment like the offerings of the "Mosquito Network"

March 1945—We managed to pick up a radio at Manus. The radios in the radio shack were intended for guarding certain frequencies—messages from the fleet and other ships. The new one, with long-wave broadcast band and two short-wave bands, could pick up programs for listening—news, music, and other entertainment.

Nearly every port now had a local station operated by the Army or Navy, and this new radio let us receive the broadcasts and relay them to the rest of the ship.

At last we could listen to many American broadcasts like "Information Please" and "Fibber McGee and Molly," relayed to the overseas stations by short wave or by transcriptions which were mailed to the stations. Sometimes they broadcast dance music from places like the Mark Hopkins in San Francisco.

Kemal Majid, a gunner's mate from Brooklyn, hooked up the radio, overcoming such complications as long leads for the antenna, the wiring to all the ship's loudspeakers, and a source of AC power. (Most of the ship used DC, but AC was used for the 20mm gun sights.)

Majid knew the technical side of radio. He was a black-haired Syrian who used to work in a radio shop—another example of the many odd trades and skills we had aboard.

The system also let us relay phonograph records to speakers throughout the living areas of the ship. Bill Chapman came back from the base at Manus with about 50 V-Disks produced for the government and sent to ships and stations overseas.

These were 12-inch disks of both classical and popular music, adding greatly to the variety of material on board. The pop records were by such leading entertainers as Benny Goodman and Kay Kyser. All the old favorites like "Frenesi," "Perfidia," "Begin the Beguine," "Dancing in the Dark." One of the best was Artie Shaw's "Stardust." (Since these were 78-r.p.m., each side would play for only about five minutes.)

Ralph Hart got homesick when he heard such music. Al Toll got a kick out of Sammy Kaye's introductions to vocals: "This beautiful thought tenderly expressed by little Nancy Norman" or "Out of our tattered and dusty manuscripts, this old favorite beautifully expressed by Russ Carlisle."

We obtained a trick record from the Army engineers whom we carried to Lingayen. It came from Australia and had two concentric tracks, so that it played either "Marching through Georgia" or "Dixie," depending on which track the needle landed on—or by jiggling the needle, it would switch from one to another!

Guadalcanal had become a lively member of the "mosquito network." Since we were in the area for nearly three weeks, we had a good chance to get acquainted with it. Besides states-produced shows like "G. I. Jill and her G. I. Jive," they put on some original stuff.

One of these was the "Atabrine Cocktail Hour," a program of dinner dance music coming from "the Lizard Lounge, high atop the water tower in downtown Guadalcanal." (Atabrine was the quinine substitute widely used by the land-based troops to prevent malaria.) The music would be interrupted by a commercial: "Have you had your Atabrine today?"—a spoof of the commercials we heard back home. These programs were real morale boosters.

I wondered which of the young men on mosquito network stations like this later became big stars on radio and television.

27

Busy Seabees Head for Okinawa

It's a full ship—bulldozers and road-building equipment,
gasoline, huge quantities of TNT, and all those Seabees.
They start to build a house on the truck ramp. We head for
Okinawa, nearly 3,000 miles away

March 1945—On 3 March we brought the LST across
Ironbottom Sound from Port Purvis, Florida Island, to Kukum Beach
on the north shore of Guadalcanal, so that we could take on a group
of Seabees (Navy Construction Battalion) and all their supplies for
transportation to Okinawa.

We took on 11 officers and 142 men of the 44th USN C. B. Regiment
and 71st USN C.B. Battalion on 5 October along with the typical
bulldozers and road-building equipment.

They had an enormous supply of TNT, since they had scarcely
used any on Guadalcanal. They loaded it about 20 feet deep across
the rear end of the tank deck. They also had considerable ammunition,
which they stored in a forward magazine. Their drums of 100-octane
gasoline were placed wherever space was available on the main
deck, between the vehicles and gun tubs. What a target!

I still marvel at how we could run right up onto the shore so easily and later pull off, ordinarily with little trouble. This was one of the best beaches we had found, without any surf, so the ship "stayed put."

At the post office we found they had just received a bunch of mail. We dug out 12 sacks for the *698*, then got a truck and drove the mail right into the tank deck (amid loud cheers).

Next afternoon we pulled off the beach and dropped anchor once more in Port Purvis, Florida Island. It was hot in the harbor, with all those troops in addition to our own crew. The wardroom was a busy place with our Seabee officers, whose heavy gear filled up the rooms. Ralph and I had a room with just two bunks, so we didn't share ours.

A change in our censorship regulations permitted us to mention ports of call 30 days after we had left them. We still couldn't give an itinerary in our letters or list the places in chronological order, but I was able to tell Fran we had seen numerous islands in the Philippines, from Leyte to Lingayen Gulf. I told her that the ports we had visited included Morotai, Biak, Hollandia, Finschhafen, and Eniwetok.

Gradually we were getting around to the scenes of previous war activity. Some ports which had been visited by nearly everyone in the early part of the war, such as Noumea and Sydney, were rapidly losing their importance as the war moved north and west. There were no towns around most of the new places. The Army and Navy brought their own towns with them.

When we became aware of the immensity of the whole operation and the huge area covered, it became amazing how fast the war had been moving. Of all the ports we had seen earlier, only Finschhafen had been ours a year before.

I visited Tulagi, a small, adjacent island which had also been a scene of earlier battles. I went to the Navy's welfare and recreation office and came out with 65 paperbacks (special armed services editions), two new checker boards and checker sets, and two table tennis sets. We'd have to get Stubby Green busy on a Ping-Pong table once we had space available. After some of his accomplishments, this should be nothing.

Next day I went over to Guadalcanal again, taking the ferry both ways. Bill King, one of the signalmen, and Tex Bavousett, our happy radarman, went with me. We went by way of Tulagi, waited an hour there, and got over to Guadalcanal about noon.

To our amazement the Red Cross met us at the dock, and a white-bloused Red Cross girl served coffee and doughnuts from a mobile kitchen. It was unbelievable that at this base some 2,500 miles from enemy action, free coffee and doughnuts were being passed out to the servicemen who had endured the rigorous ferry ride from Tulagi!

The chart office didn't begin to have all the charts I needed. We were expecting to go beyond the areas covered by our original portfolios, and we still had not received portfolios we had ordered from Sydney last November. Now I was trying to pick up charts one by one. The Guadalcanal office gave me some. Each one helped.

We finally got underway on the morning of 15 March, as part of LST Flotilla 23. As we headed for the harbor entrance, we looked down from the conn and noticed that the Seabees were up to something down at the truck ramp, which was now raised to main deck level. *They were building a house!* Already they were whacking together two-by-fours on the truck ramp—and our crew hadn't had a chance to put the tarpaulin cover over it! The skipper put a halt to this right away, and the cover was put in place. They could sleep on the ramp under the stars, but not in a house that might careen all over the deck.

We had started on one of our longest cruises, close to 3,000 miles. Our destination was Okinawa—barely 400 miles from the tip of Kyushu, the southernmost island of Japan. We would travel roughly northwest from 10 degrees south of the equator to 23 degrees north, pausing briefly en route at Ulithi Atoll. We were to arrive at Okinawa on Monday, 2 April, one day after L-day, when the first ships and troops would hit the beach.

We were glad to share the voyage with these can-do Seabees, who had been demonstrating American ingenuity wherever they went—even if we didn't want them to build a house on our uncovered truck ramp.

28

Where in the World Is Ulithi?

There's confusion about a "convoy." We enter Ulithi
Atoll and receive more mail and fresh provisions. A boatload
of beer and another task for Stubby Green

March 1945—We started on the first leg of the long trip to Okinawa, heading for Ulithi Atoll. Ulithi? Where in the world was Ulithi? As one of the thousands of atolls in the western Pacific, it was doubtful that one person in ten thousand had ever heard of it before the war. But in 1945 probably more ships and troops passed through Ulithi than any other port west of Pearl Harbor.

Ulithi is in the Carolines group, about 350 miles southwest of Guam and not too far from the island of Yap (our destination in the invasion that never happened). Ulithi was the atoll base that Franklin D. coyly referred to as Shangri La (not wanting to reveal its true name).

So here we were, on the rolling sea again. On the first day out I was on the conn much of the time. When sailing within sight of land, Sandy and I were always busy. Once again, Bill Chapman and I had been taken off the watch list. Bill had considerable pre-invasion work to do on publications, and I on navigation. That afternoon we had general quarters for anti-aircraft firing practice.

In the Western Pacific

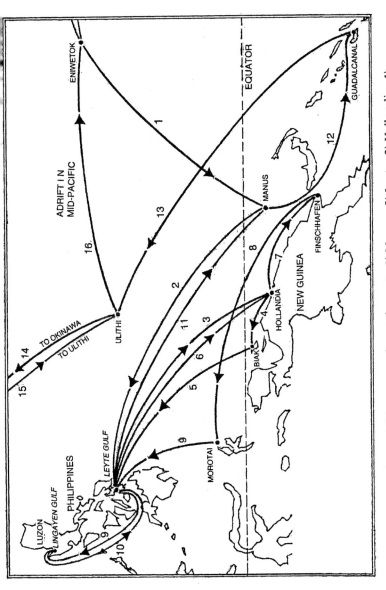

LST 698's amphibious operations take us to 1) Manus, 2) Leyte, 3) Hollandia, 4) Biak, 5) Leyte, 6) Hollandia, 7) Finschhafen, 8) Morotai, 9) Lingayen, 10) Tacloban, 11) Manus, 12) Guadalcanal, 13) Ulithi, 14) Okinawa, 15) Ulithi, 16) Eniwetok.

Shortly before hauling in the anchor at Florida Island, we had taken on a big load of fresh provisions. For the first time since we left Eniwetok last September, we had loaded up with eggs, oranges, grapefruit, and other fresh foods. Our breakfasts looked brighter.

I showed the first pictures of our new son Bill to Max Heppner, from New York City, one of our cooks. He showed me pictures of his little daughter, now eight months old, and I couldn't get over how much a child grows in that first year.

Our Seabee passengers were not to be denied their house. On Sunday at our church service on the truck ramp, we looked over what our passengers had built. After having torn down the first effort, because we had not yet drawn a tarpaulin cover over the boat ramp, they built another that turned out to be a neat, watertight job of wood and canvas. With the rain we'd been getting recently, they were glad to have it.

We had a shift in personnel. Ralph Hart became the first lieutenant, Al Toll his assistant, and Bill Eklund the assistant communications officer. The first lieutenant is in charge of the deck division, with more men under him than any of the other officers. He is responsible for the ship's upkeep, the handling of mooring lines, anchor chain, etc.

The weather continued to be overcast much of the time. Only once had we been able to get star sights since we left port. But one day the sun came out at noon (local apparent noon), and we finally got a fix. We eventually sailed away from the rain belt and had good weather again.

As we approached Ulithi on 24 March, I got up at 0530 only to find that it was pouring. Visibility was practically zero. Our convoy was making emergency turns to avoid another convoy. Eventually Tex (the radarman) and I discovered (as did the guide ship), that the "convoy" we had picked up on radar was actually ships in the Ulithi harbor! Those ships were not moving an inch! But *we* had been, and this monkey business had put us on the wrong side of the atoll. We had to spend the rest of the morning getting to the entrance on its west side.

We finally pulled into Ulithi. It was huge! Once inside we couldn't begin to see the border of tiny islands in a ring about 20 miles north to south and 14 miles east to west, providing anchorages for hundreds of ships. The entire base was on the water—supply ships, repair ships, everything except for a tiny airstrip and a place for liberty (on the island of Mogmog).

As soon as we dropped anchor, an LCM came alongside with sacks of letters for our ship and for the troops aboard.

Our yeoman, Lynn Martin, and our leading signalman, Dick Hannon, were excited to receive orders admitting them to V-12 school in Princeton. They immediately began packing their seabags and left the ship without delay. Sandy had arranged transportation for them by air, and they would have some leave before reporting on May 1.

For the rest of us, the chief pleasures were the rapid mail service and the sight of another boatload of fresh provisions—more potatoes, oranges, and genuine United States meat.

Sunday was Palm Sunday, and Art Cave, the cook, held church service. One of our passenger officers gave a sermon. It wasn't exactly a Palm Sunday service, since we sang the "Old Rugged Cross" as usual! We had very good roast chicken for Sunday dinner. The recent batch of chickens had been some of the best. (I was sorry I couldn't say the same about the Australian lamb.)

We had fine music on our new radio. At noon we heard a rebroadcast of the Cleveland orchestra playing the *Romeo and Juliet Overture* and an hour of the Metropolitan Opera.

Next day one of our LCVPs came back with a whole boatload of cans of beer. It was on a cargo net in the boat, and our portable crane lifted the whole load at once. But when the operator swung the boom around to set the load down, the boom twisted 90 degrees and crashed onto the deck. Fortunately, not a drop of beer was lost. But it was another welding job for Stubby Green. The crane was good as new the next day.

Around nine o'clock, a boat came alongside with more mail. One letter to me was dated 27 January. It looked as if it had followed *LST 698* all over the western Pacific and been dunked in the bay at each port!

On the following day we were on our way once more—for Okinawa.

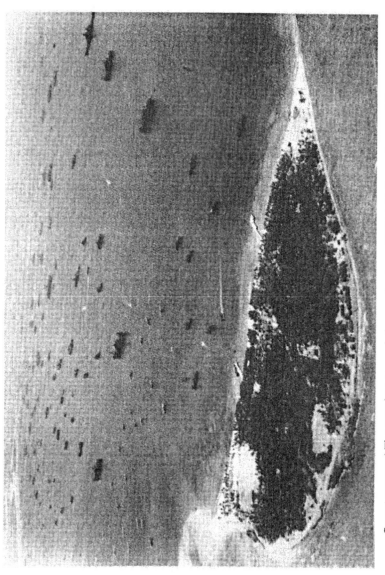

Secret weapon! The vast but scarcely known harbor of Ulithi Atoll, southwest of Guam, provided a cozy anchorage to top off fuel and supplies for hundreds of vessels sailing to and returning from Okinawa. FDR referred to it as "Shangri La." *National Archives.*

29

In Kerama Retto without a Chart

The ships roll and the weather turns cool. Easter dinner comes a day early. We sail into Kerama Retto, seized the previous week. I try to navigate without a chart. A kamikaze hits a nearby LST

April 1945—After the Philippines, we naturally began to think: What's next? One day some time back the skipper and I had been poring over a chart of the western Pacific. He put his finger down on a fairly large island in the chain that stretched roughly from the tip of Kyushu to Formosa (now Taiwan).

Okinawa. How many of us had ever heard of it? (That was nothing new to us in these little-known parts of the Pacific.)

I had checked at that time and discovered that we had no chart portfolio for that area. We had ordered it, but who knew when it would arrive? I began to scrounge for charts at Navy chart depots, first in Manus, then Tulagi and Guadalcanal.

We knew practically nothing about Okinawa, and the most impressive item in the troops' guidebooks was that there were lots of snakes. I never found out whether that was true or not.

Our LSTs, among the slowest ships, were among the earliest to pull out from Ulithi for Okinawa. Convoys were already under way from more distant staging areas like Manus, Hollandia, and Leyte. Before long the sea would be full of ships on their way to the largest Pacific invasion in World War II. Okinawa was expected to be the last major stepping stone before the landings on the Japanese mainland itself.

Some 1,213 ships and craft were employed in the amphibious phases of this operation, "including 187 of the handy, ubiquitous and greatly wanted LST," according to naval historian Samuel Eliot Morison.[1] Far more ships than at either Leyte or Lingayen. Morison pointed out that this number did not include, for example, 88 carriers, battleships, cruisers, destroyers, and escort vessels of Task Force 58. Assault troops, he said, numbered "2,380 of the Navy, 81,165 of the Marine Corps, and 98,567 of the Army."

Our own task unit included 21 LSTs, plus flagship and screen—essentially the group of ships assembled in the Guadalcanal area with us—augmented by three more LSTs.

Two days out from Ulithi the sea began to roll like nothing we had seen before. Our course put us right in a trough for mile after mile. You had to be an expert to hold your coffee cup so that it wouldn't spill.

We adapted to the rolling, but it was somewhat hard to sleep. I couldn't sleep on my back, where the motion pushed my stomach back and forth. Instead I turned over and wedged my elbow and knee between the mattress and the side of the bunk. So long as I could anchor myself down in some way, I was O.K.

The weather had been cool and comfortable. If it weren't for the rolling, these would have been good nights for sleeping, at least until 0445 each morning, when we rolled out for general quarters.

Our recreation radio now worked well at sea. The Philippine Hour was being broadcast from Manila rather than Australia. We could also get news direct from the powerful armed forces station in San Francisco.

On 31 March we had an Easter feast—a day early, because the first landings on Okinawa were scheduled for the next day. We started with hors d'oeuvres of sardines and salmon. Then steaks two inches thick! Plus French fries, corn, peas, bowls of olives, and ice cream with fudge sauce. Before the ice cream, Sandy and I had gone up to shoot stars. But we waited until later to work out our positions and plot them. The ice cream came first.

On Easter Sunday, 1 April, we had church services forward on the truck ramp, under the Seabees' tarpaulins. We knew that thousands of marines and soldiers were at that instant landing on Okinawa. It must have been a strange kind of Easter for them. We sang, "Christ the Lord has risen today." It dragged a little and sounded queer.

Typical church service was held on the truck ramp
in the shadow of a gun tub.

We noticed the difference in climate as we sailed north. The men standing outdoor watches were issued heavy fur-lined jackets. Actually, it was about 73 degrees, but it really seemed cold. Winds were blowing a spray of salt air and mist into our faces, and metal surfaces felt damp and cool.

On Monday, 2 April, we arrived in Okinawa waters. I got up at four to begin navigation and spent much of the rest of the day on the conn. We were routed to Kerama Retto, a group of small islands about 15 miles to the west.

These islands had been seized the previous week, ahead of the main event on Okinawa, with very minor U.S. casualties. Morison commented: "This neat though complicated landing took the Japanese by surprise; they never imagined that Kerama would interest us."[2]

Capt. Walter Karig's *Battle Report, Volume V, Victory in the Pacific,* reported: "The Kerama group would serve the major operation as a logistics base, protected anchorage, seaplane base, and a graveyard for kamikazed ships."[3]

Here we found a peaceful harbor, roughly seven by 13 miles, sheltered by small, rocky islands. We sailed in and out, around various islands, and dropped anchor shortly after noon. Already PBMs (Mariner seaplanes) were using Kerama Retto as an aircraft base.

However, on *LST 698* we had a novel problem in navigation. Our charts had been good up to this point, and we had a fine one of the main island, Okinawa Shima, on which our quartermaster, Al Clingen, had drawn in the various landing beaches. But without a complete portfolio for this region, we had only charts I had scrounged from chart offices.

We had no chart at all for Kerama Retto! We had that "travel folder" put out by the U. S. information services, the one that told about snakes. And on the inside back cover, there was a small map of the islands of Kerama Retto. I taped it to the chart table, and it worked.

We began to get Tokyo Rose and Radio Tokyo (in English, of course). The Japanese accounts of the invasion of Okinawa were quite different from the U. S. news broadcasts from San Francisco. Tokyo reported sinking with their aircraft some 147 of our ships! Our broadcasts, on the other hand, told how the invasion had proceeded as rapidly as planned, with light losses.

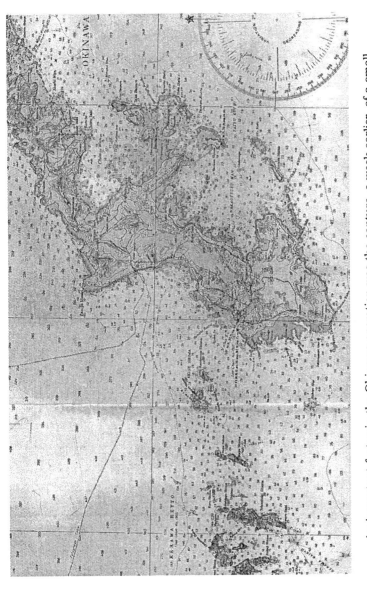

An important factor in the Okinawa operation was the capture, a week earlier, of a small group of islands known collectively as Kerama Retto (far left), some 25 miles west of Okinawa. This served as a handy anchorage and also as a seaplane base. *H. O. 2338.*

The kamikazes hit one of our ships *(LST 599)* in Kerama Retto on 3 April. At 0727 our fire and rescue party went to their aid, returning at 1030. Ensign Ralph Hart, our first lieutenant, told me recently that when they reached the ship, the fire had been brought under control but that they laid off from the ship to assist as needed. The log of *LST 599* showed that seven of the 21 injured were hospitalized, while the remainder were treated for minor injuries and discharged to duty.[1]

Morison reported:

> LST 599, carrying the gear for a Marine flight squadron, took on an attacking plane under fire at about 0715 and clipped off one wing, but the plane crashed and penetrated her main deck. where it exploded and started fires. The Marine squadron lost most of its gear and 21 men were wounded, yet nobody but the kamikaze pilot was killed.[5]

One important note: The American invaders discovered and seized some 350 suicide boats[6] which would have been used against our ships during the landings on Okinawa. They also discovered Baka suicide *bombs* which could be carried on the underside of a plane and released, with the "pilot" guiding it into the target! These weapons, once seized by our forces, could not be used against us.

During the day and a half we stayed in Kerama Retto, we received more fresh provisions. Imagine how our Seabees felt when they received oranges, bacon and fresh eggs for breakfast! Finally, on Wednesday, 4 April, we got underway for Green Beach II on Okinawa.

Notes

[1] Morison, Samuel Eliot: *History of United States Naval Operations in World War II, Volume XIV, Victory in the Pacific, 1945,* Little, Brown and Company, New York, 1975, 108

[2]   *Ibid.,* 123

[3]   Karig, Capt. Walter, USNR, Lt. Comdr. Russell L. Harris, USNR, and Lt. Comdr. Frank A. Manson, USN: *Battle Report, Volume V, Victory in the Pacific,* Rinehart & Co., Inc., New York, 1949 (Henry Holt and Company, New York), 364

[4]   *LST 599* deck log, 3 April 1945

[5]   Morison, *op. cit.,* 177-78

[6]   Nichols, Major Chas. S, Jr., USMC, and Harry I. Shaw, Jr.: *Okinawa: Victory in the Pacific,* Historical Branch, G-3 Division Headquarters, U. S. Marine Corps, 1955, 38

30

How We Wrecked Our Ship

Underwater coral reefs and strong tides at Okinawa make beaching both tricky and hazardous. With our ship hung up on an outlying reef through the night, the pounding surf causes severe damage to both engines and both shafts, making the ship inoperable—even before we unload

1 Apri 1945—First a bit about the landings at Okinawa, which began on Easter Sunday morning, 1 April (Love-Day). Some 1,300 vessels gathered off the Hagushi beaches on the western shore of Okinawa. The northern portion of these beaches was assigned to the Marines' III Amphibious Corps, the southern beaches to the Army's XXIV Corps.

Historians Jeter A. Isely and Philip A. Crowl presented this picture in their 1951 book, *U. S. Marines and Amphibious War:*

> It was a weird assemblage. Battleships, cruisers, and destroyers were stepping up their fire to fever pitch. Before the first troops touched the shore, the navy had let loose a total of almost 45,000 rounds of shells, 33,000 rockets, and 22,500 mortars. Through the din and smoke, vessels carrying the first waves of landing troops slowly felt their way to their assigned positions, dropped their stern anchors, and came to

rest fronting a shore line more than seven miles in length. These were strange craft that would have shocked any honest sailor ten years before—ungainly, flat-bottomed, scrofulous with varicolored paint. They were the tank landing ships (LSTs) and their smaller sisters the medium landing ships (LSM) both with double doors fitted into their bows almost flush with the water line. As the doors swung open, out swarmed hordes of another singular craft, the tracked landing vehicle (LVT), one of the few truly amphibians of the war.[i]

In *Storm Landings,* historian Joseph H. Alexander tells us:

> Operation Iceberg . . . got off to a roaring start on Love-Day. The enormous armada, assembled from ports all over the Pacific, now stood coiled to project its landing force over the beach. This would be the ultimate seaborne forcible entry. The epitome of all the amphibious lessons learned so painstakingly from the crude beginnings at Guadalcanal and North Africa . . .[2]

But this scene is being watched by others. In his extraordinary book, *The Battle for Okinawa,* Colonel Hiromichi Yahara gives us a strange eyewitness account from the Japanese viewpoint:

> At this time the commanders of Japan's 32nd Army are standing on the crest of Mount Shuri near the southern end of Okinawa's main island, quietly observing the movements of the American 10th Army. The commanding general of 32nd Army, Lieutenant General Mitsuru Ushijima, stands tall and composed, a fine figure of a man. The short, stout officer standing nearest to him, legs set defiantly apart, is his chief of staff, a man known for his fierce valor, Major General Isamu Cho. Ushijima's staff officers, binoculars in their hands, gaze calmly at the Kadena western shoreline, about 20 kilometers to the north . . .
>
> . . . At 8:00 A.M. the enemy infantry disembarks from the thousand-odd landing craft, thrusting onto the shore.

The sweep of the ordered military formation is impressive. It is as if the sea itself were advancing with a great roar . . .

. . . The group simply gazes out over the enemy's frantic deployment, some of the officers joking, a few casually lighting cigarettes. How could this be? For months now the Japanese army has been building its strongest fortifications on the heights of Mount Shuri—and its adjacent hills. Here they will lure the American forces and confound them. Hence their air of nonchalance. The battle is progressing exactly as expected. All the Japanese command need do is await the completion of the enemy's landing at Kadena and watch them finally head southward . . . [3]

At 1600 on 1 April, Admiral Turner sent a summary to Admirals Spruance and Nimitz: "Landings on all beaches continued, with good progress inland against light opposition. Beachhead has been secured . . . Approximately 50,000 troops have landed over beaches . . . Unloading supplies over Hagushi beaches commenced, using LVTs, DUKWs, LSMs and LSTs."[4]

*　　*　　*

4 April—Now let's proceed with the story of our *LST 698:*

On 4 April, as we approached the Hagushi beaches on the western side of Okinawa, we saw American trucks rolling over the narrow roads and noticed the locations of future camps.

Our slot at Green Beach II was a tricky place to beach. Dangerous underwater coral reefs surrounded the island. Tides played an important role, since the tide at high water was often five feet higher than at low water. An LST had beached successfully in our assigned slot the day before, and our group commander brought that ship's skipper aboard to provide first-hand information. But our LST had a deeper draft.

At 0905 on 4 April we hit the "beach" (in this case the coral reef some 400 yards offshore). The tide was at its highest level, and the ship rested on the reef about two-thirds to three-quarters of the way back from the bow. The ship was unstable, and we retracted almost immediately. We beached again at 1059. This position, too, was unsatisfactory. But this time we were unable to pull off. We were in trouble.

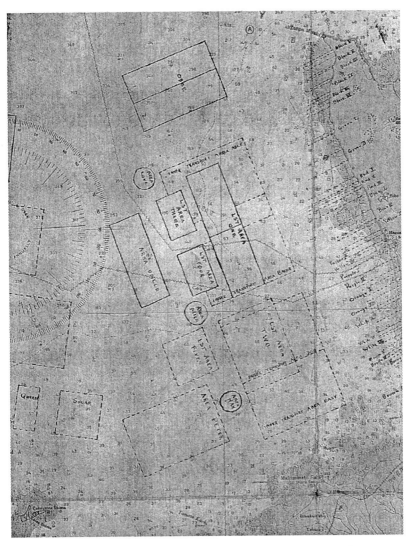

The beaches on the west shore of Okinawa, south of Zampa Misaki, presented a different hazard—outlying coral reefs. These varied in depth below the surface as did the draft of each LST. It proved to be our nemesis. *H. O. 6132.*

Another ship tried to pull us off, and the six-inch manila line fouled our port screw. Ensign Al Toll described the scene in a recent letter to the author:

> We put down several small boats to haul out a huge hawser to an ocean tug standing by. Somehow the hawser became entangled in the [port] screw and the engine simply died. I volunteered to dive under water with my trusty knife and scabbard. After what seemed ages I managed to cut the line loose and disentangled what was still around the screw. Captain Gilbert rewarded me with a small bottle of "medicinal" brandy.

The sea became heavier as we remained beached (and stranded) on the coral. Our ship creaked and groaned as it pounded heavily upon the reef. At 2050, the ship's log reported, the bedplates under the starboard and port engines began to buckle. Lines to the lube oil filter broke, disabling the starboard engine. Then at 2155 the sharp pinnacle of the reef disabled the port engine. The wind was strong and the surf increasing.

5 April—Early next morning, the tug *Tekesta* (ATF 93) dropped anchor 300 feet off our port quarter and commenced passing a two-inch cable over to our ship to pull us off the reef. By 1050 we were free of the reef, and we anchored offshore, where we remained for 24 hours.

Since we could no longer use either engine and were still fully loaded, *LST 767* moored to our port side and powered both ships side-by-side back onto the reef. Then *LST 798* joined us, beaching along our starboard side, and *LST 478* beached close aboard the port side of *LST 767*. The four ships were moored together for greater stability in unloading. They also made a bigger target for the enemy.

We learned the Japanese were sending a huge armada of aircraft to knock out our ships and beachhead positions.

By 1700 our stern began pounding once more on the coral reef. This damaged the port shaft. A hot-water pipe in one compartment bent and started to leak. The boiler was secured. Protruding cleats welded on the sides of the ships on either side of us (previously used for hauling pontoon causeways) began to pound into our hull.

Using our tide tables, I prepared a table showing the height of water above the coral each hour, based on a sounding from our bow ramp at high tide. Thus the troop officers knew when to expect waters to be low enough for unloading, and how long to expect such conditions. Finally, at 2115 we began to unload vehicles. Those Seabees worked furiously and removed all 64 of their vehicles from the ship before the tide got too high.

Getting the vehicles from our bow ramp to the shore was a problem in itself. The beach was about 400 yards away, and the hard coral bottom beneath the surf was extremely irregular.

On the beach between our ship and the shore only one or two spots of coral came above the surface at low tide; most places the water was a foot or so deep. At low tide vehicles could run over our bow ramp and make a circuitous path across the coral to the beach. Deep spots were marked with flags. Men waded out ahead of the vehicles as they inched their way to the beach.

Our procedure was to start with a tracked vehicle towing two or three trucks. This seemed to work, and we watched as trains of vehicles of all kinds wound their way to the shore.

Then at 2300 we commenced unloading bulk cargo into "alligators" or LVPs for transport to shore. These LVPs, also called "amphtracs," *swam* across the water from shore, climbed the ramp, drove into the tank deck, and loaded up. They even carried the jeeps, one at a time, saving them from being soaked. The Seabees were skilled at running these huge machines, which practically filled the bow-door opening. They even drove them up the truck ramp to the main deck and back down again. The LVPs saved many man-hours. (We knew, having unloaded ammunition at Leyte the hard way, carrying it the length of the tank deck to load it into small boats.)

Our bulk cargo was unloaded by 1500 next afternoon, and all Seabee officers and personnel disembarked. At 1600, riding much higher in the water after being relieved of all that cargo, our LCVPs towed us from the reef, and we dropped anchor once more off Green Beach 2.

We all heaved a sigh. We were glad to be rid of that huge quantity of TNT stowed in the after end of the tank deck, plus the Seabees' ammunition in our magazines, and the drums of 100-octane gasoline on the main deck.

The Seabees had been almost stymied by a large refrigeration unit on our tank deck. They were ready to let us keep it. But after we had pulled off the beach and anchored, they sent an LVP out to the ship. With our crane we lifted the "reefer" up through our cargo hatch, over the side, and down into the LVP. At last they had a place to cool their beer.

Careful examination of our ship revealed far more damage than at first realized. The official report compiled by our commanding officer[5] outlined six main areas of machinery damage, including sprung bed plates for both port and starboard engines. Both engines and both main shafts were out of alignment.

The report also listed similar damage to the frame members and plates, including the longitudinal keel member amidships. Athwartships members under the main engines bent upwards. Deck plates were sprung and many were buckled. Third-deck compartments, port and starboard, had shell plates and vertical frame members that buckled. Two tanks were taking water slowly. (Just a few of the items—see details in "Report of Damage to U.S.S. LST 698," in Appendix.)

The action report of the commander of Task Force 53.7 reported:

> LSTs *698* and *1000* suffered material damage while beaching, details of which are covered by Enclosures B-1 and C-1 respectively. It is the opinion of the group commander that no negligence on the part of the commanding officers of those ships was involved, and that the damage was due to hazardous beaching conditions.
>
> All ships which were required to beach suffered punctures of some ballast tanks, rendering those tanks unusable in some cases.[6]

Fortunately, we weren't troubled by any sort of enemy action from shore. By the time the Seabees reached the beach, the

Marines had pushed all the way across the island and north as far as Zampa Misaki, the point of land marking the northern extremity of our beaches. Yontan airfield had been captured almost immediately and was being used by our planes in 24 hours. It was great to see those Corsairs, Hellcats, and Avengers come up over the hill as they took off.

We later learned of the Japanese strategy, mentioned earlier, to hold fire and remain in caves and other protected areas as they watched our forces swarm ashore.

We did see more Japanese planes than we saw in the Philippines. We had about seven hours of general quarters on the day that some 250 or so Japanese planes were shot down. Yet we saw only eight of these planes in the distance from time to time. None broke through the navy's anti-aircraft screen to reach our ships in the unloading area.

*   *   *

6 April—The Japanese released the full power of their forces. Naval historian Morison relates:

> Admiral Toyoda, commanding all Japanese air forces in the East China Sea sector, managed in the first week of April to begin *Ten-Go* in earnest. The numbers assembled fell short of his plan, which called for a total of 4,500 aircraft, but the 699 (355 of them kamikazes) available for 6 and 7 April inflicted a distressing amount of damage. This was the first of ten massed kamikaze attacks to which the Japanese gave the name *kikusui* "floating chrysanthemums."
>
> . . . Nothing happened until afternoon [when] C.A.P. [central air patrol] shot down four planes which had been pursued from over Ie Shima. Up there a general air melee was going on, and minesweepers were catching it on the surface. By 1710 the transport area off the Hagushi beaches was ablaze with anti-aircraft fire. About five enemy planes got through the C.A.P. and four were shot down by the ships . . . [7]

Our log reported at 0505 that a single-engine enemy fighter plane was sighted at two miles. But it turned away before coming within range.

The first ships the kamikazes saw were the destroyers in the radar picket stations. The destroyer screen's anti-aircraft fire shot down many kamikazes, but those that survived dropped down out of the sky to crash on these ships. Closer in, near the invasion beaches, our fighter planes patrolled against planes that made it past the screen. We were in the center of miles of ships, and so we often spotted antiaircraft fire without even seeing the planes.

By the end of the second day, Japanese planes had hit 23 ships. Nearly all of these were among our gunfire support screen, radar pickets and fast attack groups. Six U.S. ships were sunk and four more damaged so badly that they were scrapped. American casualties from these hits were 485 killed and 582 injured. But almost none of the planes got through to our landing operations.

Meanwhile, another threat emerged, some 250 miles to the north. At 1745 on 6 April, two U.S. submarines made radar contacts of ships that had just emerged from the Bungo Suido entrance to Japan's Inland Sea, moving southwest (towards Okinawa) at 25 knots.

For this mission, Admiral Ito had his flagship, the super battleship *Yamato,* light cruiser *Yahagi,* and eight destroyers.

Colonel Yahara provided a vivid picture:

> The *Yamato* had been given only enough fuel for a one-way trip. The huge, sleek, oddly graceful ship raced south through the Bungo Straits toward the Ryukyus at flank speed. In addition to having the world's heaviest naval guns, the *Yamato* also was the world's fastest battleship. But for its last run, Imperial Headquarters could provide no air cover whatsoever.
>
> The *Yamato* was attacked by swarms of American carrier aircraft from Task Force 58 on April 6. She finally sank on the morning of the seventh, after having taken nine torpedoes and several bomb hits. The cruiser *Yahagi* and most of the destroyers in the accompanying screen were lost as well. Almost the whole crew perished, with only 200 survivors . . . [8]

The dead included Vice Admiral Ito, the attack force commander; Rear Admiral Arriga, captain of the *Yamato;* and two of three destroyer division commanders.

*   *   *

We have reported only a small part of the first few days of the Okinawa operation. We refer again to Colonel Yahara's report:

> On the land the fighting told a different story. Five days after the successful landing, the two lead divisions of U.S. XXIV Corps, soon followed by the 1st Marine Division, ran into the heavily fortified Japanese line. For the next two weeks the war settled down to the most bitter, ruthless kind of hand-to-hand fighting, as GIs and marines desperately tried to claw their way up heavily defended rocky escarpments. The advancing troops were exposed not merely to constant mortar, machine gun, and rifle fire, but they took a pounding from General Wada's artillery. It was the worst fighting of the Pacific War, its sustained intensity surpassing even the brutal combat of Tarawa, Peleliu, and Iwo Jima.[9]

Williamson Murray and Allen R. Millett put it in perspective in *A War to be Won: Fighting the Second World War:*

> As Ushijima planned, his protracted defense, lasting from 1 April to 22 June 1945, with two more weeks of "unofficial" combat, proved harrowing for the Fifth Fleet as well as the Tenth Army. In the Fifth Fleet alone, almost 5,000 died and more than 7,000 were wounded—more casualties than the U. S. Navy had suffered during the entire Pacific War over the preceding two years. The numbers for the Tenth Army were even more horrendous. To kill more than 110,000 Japanese soldiers and Okinawa auxiliaries, the Tenth Army lost 7,613 dead and missing and almost 32,000 wounded, while 26,000 fell to accidents and disease . . . [10]

149

. . . The U.S. Navy lost 64 ships sunk or so badly damaged they never returned to service; another 60 took enough damage to force extensive repairs.[11]

Morison remarked:

Sobering as it is to record such losses, the sacrifice of these brave men is brightened by the knowledge that the capture of Okinawa helped to bring Japanese leaders face to face with the inevitable, and that their surrender in August saved many thousand more Americans from suffering flaming death in an assault on the main islands of Japan.[12]

I should add that hundreds, perhaps thousands, of American servicemen who were on Okinawa and survived owe their lives to the defenses put up by American ships and planes.

On *LST 698*, we were lucky. In eleven months' time and three invasions the worst casualty on our ship had been a seaman who had caught his thumb in a hatch. But as mentioned in chapter 10, we had issued one Purple Heart, for what turned out to be a minor shrapnel wound.

*   *   *

We transferred one of our LCVP small boats to *LST 767,* and we refueled some smaller craft. Then on 10 April, we were towed back to a berth in Kerama Retto.

We had successfully delivered 152 officers and men and 584 tons of cargo. But we had disabled our ship in the process. Until our two engines and other items were repaired or replaced, we could travel only with the aid of tugs.

Notes

[1] Isely, Jeter A. and Philip A. Crowl: *The U. S. Marines and Amphibious War,* Princeton University Press, Princeton, N.J., 1951, 15-16

2   Alexander, Joseph A.: *Storm Landings: Epic Amphibious Battles in the Central Pacific,* Naval Institute Press, Annapolis, 1997, 154-5

3   Yahara, Colonel Hiromichi: *The Battle for Okinawa,* copyright, 1995, Pacific Basin Institute. This material is used by permission of John Wiley & Sons, Inc., New York, xi-xiv

4   Morison, Samuel Eliot: *History of U. S. Naval Operations in World War* II, *Volume XIV, Victory in the Pacific,* Little, Brown and Company, New York, 1975, 154

5   War Damage Report from Commanding Officer, *USS LST 698,* to Commander in Chief, U.S. Fleet, dated 7 April 1945

6   Action Report—Occupation of Okinawa Jima, Nansei Shoto, from Commander Task Group 53.7 (Captain W. W. Weeden, Jr., USN, Commander LST Flotilla 23 to Commander in Chief, U. S. Fleet, dated 18 April 1945)

7   Morison, *op. cit.,* 181

8   Yahara, *op. cit.,* 33

9   *Ibid.*

10   Murray, Williamson, and Allen R. Millett: *A War to be Won: Fighting the Second World War,* The Belknap Press of Harvard University Press, Cambridge, Mass., copyright 2000 by the President and Fellows of Harvard College, 514

11   *Ibid.,* 515

12   Morison, *op. cit.,* 282

31

President Roosevelt Dies

In Kerama Retto the word comes quietly. In office since 1933, Roosevelt was the only president many of our younger sailors had ever known. We return to Ulithi Atoll, but this time we're under tow

April 1945—Now that our ship was unloaded, we had a few relatively quiet days. Though we were at anchor, we maintained two-officer watches, because of our being in a battle area. However, we hadn't seen Japanese planes for several days.

We had the ship to ourselves after more than a month of having the Seabees with us. They were a really nice bunch, and we had enjoyed them. Now we were waiting around, wondering what they'd do with us—a fine, healthy crew and a disabled ship.

On 10 April we were towed back to Kerama Retto by AN 59, and dropped anchor in the harbor.

At Kerama Retto until now I hadn't left the ship. All our business, which wasn't much, was with other ships in the harbor. This time I jumped into a boat and took a bunch of outgoing mail to the ship which served as Fleet Post Office. I learned that some mail was coming here now to various ships, but the ships were in several areas and it was a job to get the mail to the right place—especially when ships moved around as we did. I made sure the Post Office had us down for the new anchorage.

As you might guess, I came back with a roll of charts under my arm, including a brand new anchorage chart of Kerama Retto. No more navigating from a page of the guide book.

It was quite different to ride around in a small boat here compared with tropical harbors like Hollandia and Manus. I put on a heavy sweater and then my heavy foul-weather suit, both pants and jacket. Then a raincoat because of the spray.

*   *   *

On the morning of 13 April we received word of the death of President Roosevelt. Just a brief statement at first. It must have been a great shock to many of the troops in the Pacific who were not aware of his frail health. For 30 days the colors would fly at half-staff.

Roosevelt meant a lot to our men. To average 18-year-old sailors, he had been their only president since kindergarten days—the only president they'd ever known. Elected in 1932 and reelected in 1936, 1940 and 1944, he had been their president through the Great Depression and the first three years of World War II.

We all remembered his "Day of Infamy" speech on the day after the Japanese attack on Pearl Harbor, when suddenly we found ourselves at war.

Next morning the scene changed quickly. Our LST was underway. Two LSMs (landing ships medium) came up and moored, one to starboard and one to port, and they towed us to the *LST 693*. We took a towline from the *693*, and the LSMs let go of all lines. Once again under tow, we joined a convoy bound for Ulithi.

Our ship had almost sailed without me. Our sailing orders came the night before. Bark made a quick trip to drop off remaining outgoing mail, and I rescued two of Sandy's blue suits which I had taken to a tailor shop on a seaplane tender, so that he could have his new lieutenant stripes sewed on. When we got back, our boat was lifted right up on the davits and the ship was on its way. I had never before been in a boat when it was hoisted.

Surprisingly, we found the open sea as calm as we had ever seen it. We were on virtually the same track we had covered before, which had proved so rough and rolling all the way, but in the opposite direction.

The first half-hour of the Philippine Hour was devoted to President Roosevelt, with statements from Churchill, Nimitz, and others. Our ship had a memorial service for him on Sunday, the 15th. Nearly everyone who was not on watch was present.

We discovered that out in the Pacific, away from the campaigning, we had not learned much about Truman. The thing most of us recalled was his playing the piano for Lauren Bacall while she sat on the piano and dangled her legs over the side.

We assumed that Roosevelt's death would have no affect on what we were doing in the Pacific.

32

At Ulithi, We Await Our Fate

Liberty on beautiful Mogmog. Our tank deck becomes a basketball court. The war in Europe ends. The captain flies to Hawaii, and Sandy takes over. Passengers come aboard. Our destination: Pearl Harbor

April 1945—The trip from Kerama Retto to Ulithi seemed at first like a vacation cruise, because we were under tow. No throbbing of the engines and no diesel smoke. Fortunately, we *did* have use of our auxiliary engines, which provided lights, ventilation, and use of all the machinery. We cut our watches down to a minimum, including just one officer on the conn instead of two.

That euphoria of quiet ended abruptly. There was more rust, and the men returned to chipping and painting. The chipping hammers and paint scrapers banged away all day, chipping the rust and paint scales off the main deck.

It was hard, dirty work, and the noise was something horrible. But at last it resulted in a handsome green deck—main deck and quarterdeck, navigation bridge and signal bridge. Since the hull had been given another camouflage at Guadalcanal, the ship was now well painted from bow to stern. The men were proud of their job. Whenever we tied up alongside another ship, they saw the difference. Some ships just out from the States looked run-down compared with ours.

I painted the bulkheads in our stateroom. (Ralph was busy with the deck force.) Kennedy and Chapman painted their room, Miller and Crites painted theirs, and so did the chief.

Returning southbound, we noticed it was getting warmer. A few more days and it would probably be hot again. At least we had had a change of climate for a while.

We reached Ulithi on 23 April. As usual, the main subject was mail. I got 31 letters from Fran the first day. More pictures of our new son Bill. We also got two rolls of new charts from Washington, notices to mariners, and other hydrographic information such as changes in buoys and lights, newly discovered shoals, corrections to charts. These all had to be entered in our catalogs, and, in the case of charts we expected to use soon, entered on the charts themselves.

We had no idea what would happen to us at Ulithi. Our damage, though major, could be repaired in dry dock, and we expected to be directed to an ABSD (Advanced Base Sectional Dock) like the one we had been in at Manus. Scores of ships had been damaged by kamikazes, and many of these would require dry-dock time—and perhaps not so much dry-dock time as ours. The priorities changed every day.

We had to be content to sit and wait. As it turned out, we waited more than a month in this huge anchorage bound by coral reefs and tiny islands. The largest island was just big enough for an airstrip. Another had the port director, another the recreation area. Everything else, including foodstuffs and supplies, was aboard the various ships.

Returning from a movie on another ship one evening, I turned on the radio and heard a news broadcast from San Francisco. Then classical music from Australia—"This is Anzac calling." In port we listened to the local Armed Forces station. Here we were able to pick up Guam (about 400 miles) as well as Ulithi. Once we heard the Hit Parade. Imagine Lawrence Tibbett singing "Accentuate the Positive"!

The harbor had calmed down. When we were here before, it was rough nearly all the time. Now there was scarcely a ripple. The moon was full. We saw the red sunset in the west and the rising moon in the east.

One day we took a boat over toward a coral reef. I had never seen the water so clear. We could look straight down 20 feet or more. The fish were everywhere.

Finally I went ashore—for the first time at Ulithi. I accompanied a liberty party to the "beautiful tropical isle" of Mogmog. My chief duties were to collect 25 cents from each man and buy our quota of two cases of beer and one case of Cokes. After signing various affidavits I procured the beer and Cokes, and the fellows carried them to a relatively shady spot in a grove of coconut palms.

Thousands of sailors spread out through the grove, drinking their beer and cokes and lying around. In the center was a bandstand where the "Mogmog Swingsters" were grinding out their own versions of hit parade tunes. Our men gradually drifted off to see the island. They couldn't drift far!

"Officers' Country" had three separate officers' clubs, for a) ensigns, jg's, and warrant officers; b) lieutenants, lieutenant commanders, commanders; c) captains and flag officers.

You had to buy a membership card and a book of "chits" (coupons). I had bought a 25-cent share of Cokes, so my thirst was well taken care of.

At 3:30 we all met in "berth 3," one of the markers placed near the boat landing to aid in assembling the various groups. I informed the master-at-arms that we were mustered. We heard the announcement to our boat crews, *"LST 698* lay down to the dock," and we waited for our boat to make the landing in competition with 30 or 40 others.

We took on some provisions. At Kerama Retto we had been instructed to leave all provisions in the "forward area" except for what we'd need before we reached the next port. That made sense. The supplies we received at Ulithi were fresh from the States.

One day I went on quite a boat trip with Ralph Hart and about 10 men on various errands. Ralph had business on a repair ship, Bark went for mail, and one of the men went with a pharmacist's mate to see a doctor. I did some errands for Sandy. I picked up officer messenger mail, made arrangements for a water barge to come alongside, and went to a receiving ship (a big transport) to arrange for four new seamen and an extra steward's mate to fill our quota.

While on the transport, I heard my name shouted out: "Mr. Haswell." It was Lee Voudry, our former cook from Gloversville, NY. In February, when we were in Manus, he had been transferred to the Naval Hospital because of varicose veins. Since then he had been all over the Pacific looking for us. In about ten minutes he had his papers and seabag and was on his way back to the ship with the five new men.

As we approached the 698, someone on our ship spotted him in the boat, and by the time we pulled alongside, 50 or 60 guys had lined the rail to welcome him back. Many considered him our best cook. (Before the war he had been a caterer specializing in shore dinners.) Despite his trip to the hospital ship, his varicose veins were no better than before.

Our tank deck became a basketball court, marked off with free-throw lines and everything. The shipfitters made the basketball backboards and baskets. Ralph, Monty and Crites had played basketball in college, so they were major enthusiasts. Plenty of fellows had fun.

With a huge open space like that, the LST was one of a kind. We had said an LST is a crazy ship. What's crazier than a warship with a basketball court?

I received an additional assignment—replacing Ray Kennedy as ship's service officer. That put me in charge of the store, barber shop, and laundry. Francis Dutch, our storekeeper from Monongahela, Pa., operated the store for about an hour each day, selling candy, gum, cigarettes, soap, cigars, and miscellaneous necessities.

The war in Europe ended. When we got the word, I wrote Fran that it would be interesting to learn the reaction in Chicago to the news. Here, where there were no newspapers and our reports came mainly by radio, the actual fact that the war was over in Europe created only casual comment. We had been amazed by the dramatic events of the past ten days in Europe—Hitler's disappearance, the swallowing up of various provinces of Germany by Allied and Soviet armies, the separate surrenders made by German generals. But such news gave us no impulse to raise general whoopee. The announcement stopped the bidding in a bridge game for about 15 seconds.

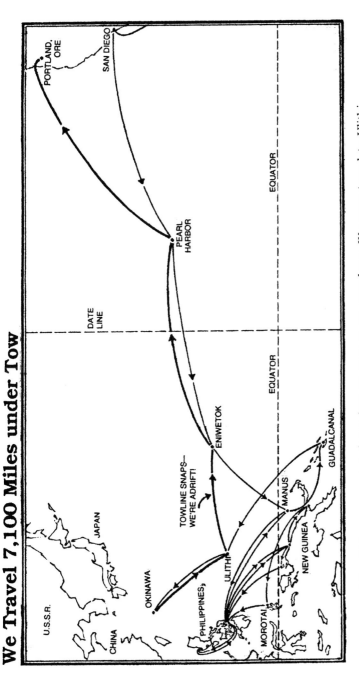

We Travel 7,100 Miles under Tow

After Okinawa we were dependent on tugs to go anywhere. We were towed to Ulithi, expecting to be repaired in an Advanced Base Sectional Dock. After 25 days they ordered us on to Pearl Harbor. We waited 34 more days and finally were sent to Portland, Ore.

We mustered the crew, and the captain announced that he was leaving the ship in the morning and that Ken Saunders (Sandy), our executive officer, would take over as captain. The captain told us he expected to rejoin us when we returned to Pearl Harbor. We had expected that would be our destination. The increasing demand for dry-dock space had made our chances here look more unlikely each day.

None of us knew beforehand about his leaving. It was quite a surprise. Sandy told me later that the skipper was to have examinations at a naval hospital. Next day the officers had an early breakfast and at 0700 the captain took a boat to the airstrip.

When Sandy became captain, Eric moved up to executive officer, and Lou Miller got Eric's job as stores officer. I continued to serve as navigator, although on an LST the executive officer officially held that title.

I went aboard the battleship *Missouri* on another trip, to get one of our passengers. Of course we didn't know then that this ship would soon be the scene of the official Japanese surrender.

Somehow, as ship's service officer I became the beer baron of *698*. One day I brought back 100 more cases. The fellows had grown tired of Mogmog. So we began having beer about every other day in the tank deck—two bottles or cans per man. They really liked the beer, and this saved taking a boat six miles each way to the island.

The work in taking over ship's service was more than I had expected. I had never had any bookkeeping or accounting, so I guessed they would get some quite unusual reports. But we were able to get good merchandise, and sales were good,

More fresh provisions. We'd eat lots of fresh produce again. It was nice to see the potato bins full of potatoes instead of cans of paint.

Mother's Day was 13 May, and I wished I could be home with Bill's mother. Our cook and "preacher," Art Cave, held services, and we also sent a boatload of men to Catholic and Protestant services on other ships. We had splendid chicken for dinner. In the afternoon I sat in the shade of the bridge and read the issue of *Time* telling of Roosevelt's death.

On 18 May we took a large group of passengers aboard. These were the crew of the *LST 884,* the ship which was to be towed with us.

The next day we finally got the two ships under tow and headed for Pearl Harbor.

33

What Happened to the *LST 884?*

In the landings at Okinawa, LST 884 was one of the
first ships to be hit and crippled by a kamikaze suicide
plane. It ripped into the 884's port side at the waterline,
starting fires and exploding ammunition

May 1945—The *LST 884,* which was towed back to Pearl Harbor
with our *LST 698,* was hit by a Japanese kamikaze suicide plane at the
very outset of the Okinawa invasion. It was assigned to Task Force
51.8, a diversionary force intended to simulate a landing on the
southeast coast of Okinawa while the main U. S. forces were landing
further north, on the west coast of the island.

(This ship had also been involved in the Iwo Jima invasion, where
it had been bombed by Japanese planes and hit by mortar fire from
Mount Surabachi.)[1]

LST 884 had left Saipan on 25 March with 300 Marines, 17 tracked
landing vehicles, 9 amphibious tractors, and 81MM and 60MM mortar
ammunition aboard.[2]

In the early hours of L-Day (Easter Sunday, 1 April 1945) the
convoy had been circling at about six knots. General quarters was
sounded on the *884* at 0521.[3] At 0548 three enemy planes were
reported in the immediate vicinity. Thirty seconds later all port guns

on the *884* opened fire on a plane bearing 270 degrees, at a height of 200 to 300 feet.

The plane instantly burst into flames, nosed into a shallow dive, and crashed into the port side of the *884* at the waterline, just forward of the superstructure. It passed through the shipfitter's shop, and on into the tank deck, where it exploded with intense flame, according to the *LST 884's* Action Report:

> The plane had crashed through the tank deck's bulkhead and through the 81MM and 60MM mortar ammunition which was stowed at this point, causing ammunition to explode. It was impossible to get into the tank deck to fight fire, due to exploding ammunition.[4]

Within seven minutes of the crash it was feared that exploding ammunition or fuel tanks would blow the ship to bits. Abandon ship was ordered. Port and starboard boats and all life rafts were lowered. By 0605 all hands were reported out of living areas and engine rooms. Men in the water were being picked up by ship's boats and boats from *LST(M) 678, LST 838,* and by *ATR 80.* The Commanding Officer went over the side at 0610 into *LST(M) 678's* small boat and was taken to destroyer *DD 656,* lying to nearby.

At about 0715, the *884's* Commanding Officer, aboard the *DD 656,* determined that most of the heavier ammunition had already been expended. He decided the ship could be saved if the fire was fought from on board. He and four other ship's officers, three Marine officers and 15 enlisted men returned to the ship.

Four support craft, the *LCSs 115, 116, 118,* and *119,* secured alongside or lay close aboard and put water on the deck. Fire and rescue parties from these ships also boarded the ship. The remainder of the crew of the *884,* aboard *LST(M) 678,* reported aboard, together with a fire and rescue party from *DD 656.* Several heavy explosions and numerous minor ones occurred during this time, according to the Action Report.

By 1100 the fire was determined under control. At 1400 *USS Yuma (AT 94)* took the ship in tow and headed for Kerama Retto, dropping anchor in the harbor at 1838.

The bodies of eight Marines were recovered from the tank deck. Nine other bodies were found without dog tags, all burned beyond recognition. One of these may have been the Japanese pilot.

But the day wasn't over. At 2239 forward sentries reported small arms fire being directed at the ship, apparently by snipers. At 2315 one man was killed and another wounded in both arms. Security was doubled.

At this point only 59 of the 109 crew members were on board. These were temporarily housed on the *Egeria (ARL 8)*, and all the perishable stores and meats on the 884 were transferred to the *Egeria*. Then on 2 April, 13 crew members who had been picked up by the A*TR 80* were returned aboard.

The ship's company, berthed on the *LST(M) 575*, began cleaning up the ship and salvaging useful gear. The crew cannibalized ordnance equipment for urgent use aboard operative ships, transferring spares to *LCI(G)s*. Two additional unidentifiable bodies were found on the tank deck.

LST 884's commanding officer learned on 13 April that the ship was scheduled to be towed the next day to Guam. Welders from the command ship *Mt. McKinley (AGC7)* immediately set out to close the large hole in the port side. Forty members of the crew were transferred to *LST 71* for berthing and messing en route south. Seven officers and 30 men remained aboard as skeleton crew. On 14 April the ship was taken in tow for Guam in company with Task Unit 51.15.21. Emergency cooking and messing facilities were established, using a gasoline pressure burner. A "Chic Sale" type toilet was built outboard from the starboard quarter.

A change in the orders diverted the ship to Ulithi, where bomb disposal experts removed the two unexploded bombs, and also the remaining unexploded cargo ammunition.

On 24 April 36 more enlisted crew members, who had been picked up by the *LST 838's* boats, returned, plus one man from *LST 812*. Three members of the crew who were unaccounted for were believed to be aboard the *DD 656*, according to the *LST 884's* Action Report.

In all, 24 sailors and Marines had been killed and 21 wounded, according to Historian Samuel Eliot Morison.[5]

Notes

[1] Letter to author from Alfred J. Geary, Sm2c, USCG, LST 884, dated 18 Aug 1999. (Geary was an eyewitness to the kamikaze hit. He was "a signalman standing on the port wing of the flying bridge, just above the wheelhouse, looking directly at the plane coming at us and then dipping into our port side.")

[2] USS LST 884 Action Report—Okinawa Operation, 27 April 1945

[3] USS LST 884 Ship's Log, 1 April 1945

[4] Action Report, *op. cit.*, 2

[5] Morison, Samuel Eliot: *History of United States Naval Operations in World War II, Volume XIV, Victory in the Pacific, 1975,* Little, Brown and Company, New York, 1975, 154

34

The Cable Snaps! We're Adrift!

At first we have calm water, like a mirror. The men play basketball on the empty tank deck. Then we run into rough seas, the cable snaps, and we're adrift. Our men work through the night preparing a new cable and bridle

June 1945—All LSTs in the Pacific had a lot of things in common. But we expect that only *LST 698* can make this claim: *We were adrift in mid-Pacific for almost 24 hours.*

After we were towed to Ulithi, we expected to be put back in service at an Advanced Base Sectional Dock. But as more and more ships competed for the use of repair facilities, our priority went steadily down.

We were restless, waiting day after day for sailing orders. When we finally received the orders, they were for Pearl Harbor. Not a tear was shed.

On 19 May we sailed from Ulithi, towed by the *SS Point Judith,* a merchant tug. Its towline was connected to the other disabled ship, the *LST 884,* and a second towline ran 800 yards from the stern of the *884* to our bow. We carried the *LST 884's* crew as passengers.

The weather was ideal. The water was calm and quiet, almost like a mirror as we glided silently through it—at five knots.

I was glad to use the sextant again after so long in port. But since this was going to be such a lengthy trip, with relatively light duties, I began to spend part of my time helping the other officers brush up on their navigation. They took star sights and sun lines and tried to remember what they had learned in officer training school. Each officer worked with me for a day.

The passengers shared watches with our crew on this trip, so the men had only one watch in seven. Our officers stood one O. D. watch out of nine. Eric's promotion to executive officer took him off the watch list.

Making quick use of the newly converted basketball court on the tank deck, the men formed teams for a tournament. They also rigged up a homemade quoits court, making the quoits rings from pieces of line. We could almost call our ship an LSR (landing ship recreation).

Our merchant tug changed time independently of us as we passed from one time zone to the next. They kept standard time, more or less. We preferred daylight saving. We even crossed the International Date Line at different times!

We just coasted along, terribly slowly. We joked that all the O.D. had to do up on the conn was to keep an eye on the towline, just in case it snapped.

Well, the weather *did* change. The sea became *much* rougher. We watched the *884* rise on the crest of a wave and then drop down, and a moment later we'd rise and fall the same way. Despite the length of tow, sometimes the movements of the two ships would produce slack. And then the line would quickly draw taut. It was a mighty heavy steel cable; could it possibly snap?

It could. And it did!

Suddenly that heavy cable no longer joined our ships! We could see one end dangling off the stern of the *884,* going straight down into the sea. Off our bow the other end did the same. *LST 884* was still attached to the tug, but we were no longer connected to anything.

Bob Crites, the O.D. at the time, reported in the ship's log for 25 May: "1312 Tow cable parted between *LST 884* and this ship. 1545 Towing cable retrieved and stopped off along rail along port side, around fantail, and up starboard side, 100 feet."

Our ship slipped into the trough of the sea, and we began to roll worse than on our trip to Okinawa.

Signals went back and forth between our ship and the tug, determining what to do. We had a spare reel of cable back on the fantail—part of our modicum of spare parts. But how could the cable be fitted out and connected to the *884*, which had no power of its own? *Our* ship's auxiliary engines were running, providing power for lights, refrigeration and such machines as our winches or capstans.

Our solution was to connect the cable directly to the tug, so that both LSTs could be towed in parallel. Our crew had to pull the cable out along the deck, fasten it at intervals to the side of the ship, and fabricate a bridle for our bow to absorb the heavy strains put on the cable by the sea. Meanwhile the tug maneuvered to keep herself and the *884* close at hand, ready to pick up our tow in the morning.

Where were we? Roughly 300 miles north of Truk, an island in the Carolines. Truk had been a large Japanese naval base in the early part of the war. We didn't know how many Japanese were still there. The next day's morning orders announced facetiously: "0800: Liberty party ashore on Truk."

Many persons worked through the night to prepare the cable and bridle. At 0745 on 26 May the *SS Point Judith* came along the starboard side to receive a messenger line thrown from our ship in order to pass the cable to her. We made no progress toward Pearl

Harbor during that 20 hours. In fact, we were set back about 35 miles.

By 0907, according to our log, we were once again underway, in tow of the *SS Point Judith* with 1,100 feet of cable between us. The tug and *LST 884* were connected by a separate tow cable about 500 feet long.

Then the log reports: "0930: *SS Point Judith* stopped, proceeded to maneuver without success to put *LST 884* astern of LST 698. 1050: *LST 698* towing cable caught in screw and rudder of *LST 884*. 1115: cable freed." The *SS Point Judith* finally got underway once more and proceeded at about 2.5 knots.

The 3rd of June was the anniversary of the ship's commissioning the year before. The cooks had been planning it for some time. The result was a feast. Art Cave roasted twenty 15-pound turkeys. He was up most of the night and came up to the conn briefly while I was on the midwatch. Lee Voudrey cooked the rest of the meal—dressing, cranberry sauce, vegetables, etc.

Cave also made a fancy cake big enough for the two crews. It was decorated with the names of our invasions. On top was a commissioning pennant made by Glenn "Tex" Bavousett. The cake was served on the main deck after dinner.

Next day we reached Eniwetok. A harbor tug maneuvered us to an anchorage and moored the *LST 884* to our port side. Then our electricians ran a power line from our ship to the *884*, in order to operate her bow anchor capstan. After we ran our stern anchor cable through the *884's* capstan, we secured the power, cast off the lines, and let the *884* drift astern on our stern anchor line.

We got underway once more on 7 June, in tow of the *SS Point Judith*. The tow was lengthened to 1,850 feet and the tow from our ship to the *LST 884* at 1,150 feet. We were prepared to complete the remainder of the trip to Pearl Harbor without further mishap.

Returning to Pearl Harbor, the crew broke out their dress whites for their first *real* liberty since they left Pearl Harbor a year before. And now, away they go!

35

Tedium Turns to Jubilation

We pass Bikini Atoll. One of our men comes down with appendicitis; we rendezvous with another ship, and he's transferred by breeches buoy. So little to do; we fly kites. At last, we reach Pearl Harbor and MAIL

June 1945—After clearing the Eniwetok harbor entrance, we headed east once more. Soon we sailed past Bikini, an atoll in the northern portion of the Marshalls.

Hardly anyone had heard of it then. Later, of course, Bikini was the scene of atomic testing. Since two-piece swimming suits were then coming on the market, bikini seemed like a logical thing to call them—although native women and girls in this part of the world might have been as happy with just the bottom, a "monokini."

This was to be a long trip—and our longest time without mail—but we were looking forward to sackfuls when we finally reached Pearl Harbor. At least we were able to drop off some outgoing letters at Eniwetok.

The weather was pleasant and comfortable. With such a mild sea, the tug pulled the two LSTs at *five* knots. That meant that in 24 hours we would cover only 120 nautical miles!

I continued to give each officer a chance to practice his navigation. It was Monty's turn one day; Lou Miller's the next, then Bob Crites' and then Ek's. These officers did most of the work, but I offered suggestions or instructions as necessary.

I worked on our inventory of navigational supplies, making sure we had made requisitions for all supplies needed when we reached Pearl Harbor. We also had to send an annual inventory of navigational instruments to Washington at the end of the fiscal year.

*　　*　　*

Suddenly we were concerned when Courtney Brown, a fireman from Warwick, R.I., came down with appendicitis. Unfortunately, this time we had no doctor aboard. A radio message requesting aid brought a reply from a ship quite distant from us. They told us to change our course and rendezvous with them next morning at a certain latitude and longitude.

I had the midwatch that night, and we picked up the ship by instruments about 0340. Soon it was close at hand, talking with us by blinker light. Since Brown was resting easily, we put off transferring him until morning.

When I got up at seven, after a sound two-and-one-half hours' sleep, the ship was about 25 yards off our starboard side, with its speed adjusted to ours. We constructed a breeches buoy with which we transferred him.

After a heavy line had been made secure between the two ships, and steadying lines had been run across, Brown was placed in a stretcher and started on his way. The other ship heaved in on the steadying lines as we slacked off on ours. He was quickly pulled across and eased onto the other ship's deck. He made it O. K., but I bet he was relieved when it was all over. The sea was reasonably calm, but nothing like a harbor.

The stretcher went across a couple of times after that, while we traded an extra blinker light and a couple of extra guns for four crates of apples and oranges, amidst good-natured bickering and wisecracks from the two captains over bullhorns. We also gave them some outgoing mail, because they'd reach port before we would. Then they cast off lines, and we went our separate ways.

Day or night the temperature was in the low eighties. Out on the sunny deck it was a different matter. Sometimes the heat seemed to come right up through our shoes.

We flew kites! Some of the passengers got the idea. There was now a fair wind. It was easy to get a kite into the air, but it would just take a couple of loops and crash into the sea. The men added more rags to the tail, but still it didn't stay up long.

Then they added even *more* rags to the tail. With that it sailed up over the boats, over the conn and up and up. They let out 1,000 feet of line. We wondered what the admirals in Washington would have said if they had known an LST was flying kites!

We had a laugh when Meatball, the dog mascot, went after the tail of the kite. We thought it might pull her right off the ship. Meatball was still a half-pint—not much larger than when we got her, but fatter. One of her best friends was Art Cave, one of our cooks. Meatball attended church with him every Sunday and ate good food from the galley.

Monty, one of our boat officers, organized some gym classes on the tank deck. No calisthenics, but basketball, volleyball, quoits, boxing, tiddlywinks, everything but curling and bowling-on-the-green. The men were divided into five one-hour periods, with Monty in charge.

We had expected the usual Navy exercises—jumping jack, windmill, squat thrusts, pushups. The idea went over better when the men found they could do what they wanted to.

They started a basketball tournament among the divisions, and this time they had uniforms. Tex Bavousett, radarman and ship's cartoonist, cut stencils, and they painted designs on their skivvy shirts. The engineers had a propeller like the one on a motor machinist's rating badge, gunnery had crossed guns, etc.

We had pizza—something most of us had never heard of in 1945. Our *LST 884* passengers had an Italian baker. Sometimes he'd bake pizza and bring it around about nine o'clock at night. It was a hit.

The author with fellow officers Monty, Al Toll, Sandy (Ken Saunders, executive officer), and Captain Glen Gilbert.

When we returned to Pearl Harbor, permission was granted to use cameras—but supplies of film were limited. Here's the author on a cool day as we approached the West Coast.

With hand-woven quoits, George Hensle shows 'em
how to toss 'em.

We kept counting the miles and hours until we'd reach port—and contemplated the number of sacks of mail waiting for us. More important than liberty or ice cream or movies, mail seemed to be the number one priority after six weeks without any of these things.

At last the day came—the 27th of June. Hawaii!

Before we even passed the harbor entrance at Pearl Harbor, we lowered a boat into the water and sent it off ahead of us to the post office. It returned before we turned from the main channel into West Loch. The boat was loaded to the gunwales. In the space where 40 men could stand, it was *filled* with mail!

I got 44 letters from Fran, all at once, plus 22 other letters, eight copies of *Time*, and various parcel post items that had never caught up with us until now.

I learned that our son Bill had had surgery for inguinal hernias at three months. Fran had wisely waited to write anything about it until Bill had recovered. She didn't want the last letter I received before leaving port to be one saying that Bill was *going into* surgery. The shock of that particularly long letter was broken by my arranging the letters chronologically and opening her most recent letters first. After learning that as of 20 June, just a week before, she and Bill were O. K., I started in at the beginning of her letters.

Two days later I was still submerged in mail. But what a wonderful feeling!

36

Hawaii—A Glorious Return!

Captain Gilbert rejoins us. We wait once more for drydock time. In the meantime, we have liberty every other day. Taxis, buses, and a narrow-gauge railway. We explore Honolulu and run into old friends

July 1945—We tied up in Pearl Harbor's West Loch, a sight familiar to us this time. As at Ulithi, we found that *LST 698* was not high on the priority list for dry-dock facilities. The greatest urgency was to prepare as many ships as possible, as rapidly as possible, for use in the invasion of Japan's mainland. Many were being fitted, for example, with missile launchers.

Captain Gilbert returned, looking well and vigorous, and resumed command. Sandy and Eric were approved for leaves and left almost immediately. Then Bob Crites was transferred for leave and reassignment. Bob had been on temporary duty orders ever since he left for Leyte last fall and had joined us at Hollandia in December. He had completed 18 months in the Pacific, operating a crash boat in the invasions of Kwajalein, Eniwetok, and Saipan before he joined us. His six men were also transferred.

At Pearl Harbor we tied up in West Loch and at last could take pictures of our *LST 698* and a couple of our boats (LCVPs).

Because of the low workload, the Captain divided the officers and men into port and starboard sections to permit each group to have liberty every other day. We would then take a boat to the base or, if we were going into Honolulu, to the boat landing. The bus to Honolulu took us past Hickam Air Force Base. We passed the Dole pineapple plant, where the water tower was shaped like a huge brown and green pineapple. We then came into the center of town. The Waikiki area was about two miles beyond.

I lost no time going on liberty with Ralph and Monty. It was a rare treat to ride in buses and actually buy a meal! At the landing we hailed a taxi. That felt funny after months of riding everywhere in Jeeps. The taxi had *shock absorbers!* When we reached downtown Honolulu, the first thing we did was go into a drug store and order ice cream. We made the usual rounds of souvenir shops, wandered here and there and eventually ended up at a hotel where we had a fine dinner. Our table was near the window, and we could hear the waves breaking beneath us.

On Sunday morning I again caught a bus for town. I wanted to go to church. I hadn't attended a genuine church service in a year. About halfway from downtown to Waikiki, I found the Central Union Church.

The church was beautiful, gray stone outside, white inside. It had big open windows on each side and open French doors beneath them that opened out onto gardens. The pews and pulpit were walnut. It was completely air-conditioned with the only air conditioning they really needed in Hawaii—fresh air. The large grounds in front of the church, beautifully landscaped before the war, had been turned into victory gardens and air-raid shelters.

A note at the bottom of the church program invited all service men and women to luncheon following the service. When I shook hands with the minister as I left, he said, "See you over at the parish house."

Soon the women of the church were serving dinner to about 250 Army and Navy officers and men, at long tables in a pleasant dining room. They had counted the servicemen during the service to know how many places to set. The meal was served cafeteria-style—meat loaf, cabbage salad, potato chips, and chocolate cake. Two hundred and fifty, we learned, was a small number compared with Christmas, Easter, etc.

After the luncheon (and a request for seven volunteers to do dishes), they took down the tables and arranged chairs near the piano. A Navy lieutenant led in singing songs like "Stardust," "Old Man River," and "Blue Hawaii" from a song booklet.

When I left, I took out my Honolulu map to see whether to go north, south, east, or west. It was a pleasant day. I decided to walk over to the university and shortly found it—a group of light stucco buildings with high bluffs behind it. Air raid shelters were everywhere.

I continued walking through residential streets. For many blocks there were no sidewalks, just grass parkways. I took a bus to Waikiki and found a good restaurant. Then I walked over to a hotel, where I bought a paper and watched the surf breaking on the beach.

Another day, I was visiting the ship's service store on the base at Pearl Harbor and ran into Myron Gordon. He was one of my friends at the University of Wisconsin and a lawyer whom I used to see at Great Lakes. For more than a year he had been at the district legal office at Pearl Harbor. He invited me to lunch the following Tuesday: "Come about 11 and bring your swim trunks."

When I joined Myron for lunch, we walked over to the officers' club's pool, which had an outdoor restaurant. We had sandwiches and a milk shake after our swim. I invited him over to the ship for supper the following night. Of course we couldn't reciprocate with a pool.

We received lots of new charts. I checked them off, indexed them and put them away, like a true map collector. The quartermaster might have done this, but I was interested in seeing what we were getting. Miscellaneous charts might cover areas in Australia, Tahiti, French Indochina, Kamchatka, and the Aleutians.

On 7 July Bill Chapman, Ray Kennedy, Monty, Lou Miller, and Ek came out with new jg bars, effective 1 July. They had been promoted from ensigns to lieutenants junior grade. (They had all received their commissions in February 1944; three months ahead of Ralph and me.)

Monty and I went swimming at the beach one day. We took a narrow-gauge railroad from the fleet landing into town. Then we caught a bus to Waikiki for a swim. It was fun to swim in the surf, except for occasional coral patches. As always, the water temperature was perfect.

181

We wandered down the beach to the Moana hotel and saw the weekly *Hawaii Calls* radio program being broadcast to the mainland. The musicians all wore bright shirts and cotton slacks. The announcer wore a blue slack suit and dark glasses. A guy in a tan slack suit and dark glasses gave the nod for applause.

Then we went back to the Royal Hawaiian and discovered a Navy dance band putting on a mid-afternoon dance. The band was really good. But the Waves didn't show up. No girls for the sailors to dance with.

We walked on to the aquarium, with its brightly colored fish, eels, and sea turtles. Then we returned to Waikiki and continued all the way to downtown Honolulu, stopping at the restaurant where I had eaten the previous Sunday. It was quite a hike but the best way to see the town.

One of our boats pulled up shortly after we got to the landing, and we rode back to a movie theater at the base, near our ship. We saw a goofy comedy and a genuine western in the open air.

I went with Bavousett and our other radarmen to a two-day radar navigation school. On the second day we went out on an LCC (about the size of a PT boat).

Monty and I took a bus around the island—a special trip for officers, sponsored by the Navy. The bus took us to a naval officers' camp on the north side of Oahu. We swam at a strip of sandy beach and then had dinner. The camp had tennis courts, cabins and a lounge, all for $1.50 a day. Continuing along the shore, we stopped at the Mormon Temple at Laie, a beautiful place with reflecting pool, terraces, and hedges.

At a roadside stand where we bought Cokes, we sat on the grass and watched a hula dance. The daughter danced barefoot on the lawn, while her mother sang and played a guitar. About 30 cameras popped out from the bus riders.

One day Al Toll came in my room with smiles all over him and announced that his girl had said, "Yes!" That brought me right back to 1942 and my feelings when Fran gave me the same answer.

Through connections of the Captain's, our officers were invited to a picnic. It was held at the home of an Army lieutenant and his family in

Kailua, across the island. We took a cattle-wagon-type, chartered Navy bus through town, past Diamond Head, and around Makapuu Point to the beach. A beautiful place. We got right into our swimsuits and into a game of volleyball. Then lunch, with ham and cheese sandwiches, potato salad, cucumbers, pie, etc.

We had some great swimming. The water was ideal. One hazard was the Portuguese Man of War, which stung half a dozen people. I hadn't seen one before. It had a peculiar jelly-like body about an inch in diameter, with string-like tentacles about four feet long, which might wrap around the victim's foot or leg. These tentacles are scarcely thicker than a spider's web—but they eject venom on whatever they touch. Fortunately, I didn't get mixed up with that fellow! We had steaks for dinner—an inch-and-a-half thick, cooked on a charcoal fire in an open fireplace.

We returned by a different route, over the Pali. Up and up and up, snaking around dozens of turns. We looked back at the lights and winding road far beneath us. At the top of the Pali, the wind blew with terrific force. The driver dropped us at the fleet landing, where we took our boat back to the LST.

Bill Chapman, Lou Miller, the chief and I went to church one Sunday at a base chapel—a large Quonset hut lined with insulation board. I returned to the LST for an afternoon watch and had two really good meals aboard—turkey at noon and creamed chicken and french fries at supper.

I had lunch with Bob Ela at last—a guy I had known since kindergarten. I hadn't seen him since January 1942. Bob was now a lieutenant, captain of a PC (patrol craft). He had previously been captain of a PC in the Caribbean and had asked for a change of duty to a larger ship. Instead he got another PC, older and dirtier than his first ship, and way out in the Pacific.

Bob had been home in December 1944, and when his leave expired, he set out to find his new command. He was sent to Manus. They hadn't heard of the ship. He flew to Ulithi, Palau and Leyte, took a transport to Lingayen and back, and finally caught up with the ship at Guadalcanal. So despite his being in the Pacific just since January, he had seen many of the ports we had seen, plus Palau.

On 26 July, after a year of trying, Lou Miller procured a motion picture projector. The crew would no longer need to go to other ships for their movies.

That news was topped within hours by word that practically all of the crew would get LEAVES! Morale on the ship went UP!

Then we learned even better news. We were *not* going into drydock at Pearl Harbor. OUR LST 698 WAS RETURNING TO THE MAINLAND!

Ek left the ship on "special temporary duty." He was sent ahead by air to the Mainland to obtain leave transportation for at least half of the officers and crew.

And on 30 July we were on our way. Destination: Puget Sound!

37

To Portland, and THE WAR ENDS

On 30 July, under tow, we set out for Puget Sound,
then change course for Portland. On 6 August,
the atom bomb drops on Hiroshima and three days
later on Nagasaki. The war ends on 14 August
as we approach Portland. We moor downtown.
At last, at midnight, I reach Fran by phone

August 1945—Yes, it actually happened. On 30 July 1945 we pulled out of Pearl Harbor with destination Puget Sound. We were towed by U.S. Army *L. T. 452*, in Convoy PR-506.

Rounding Barbers Point, Oahu, we turned north to pass to the west and north of Oahu, and we were truly on our way! Two days later, just to remind us we were still in the Navy, we conducted a fire drill, fire and rescue drill and abandon ship drill.

I tussled with the monthly ship's service report, going through the agony of trying to make the right side add up to the same figure as the left side. We had to take a complete inventory, find out how much stuff we had bought, how much we had sold, how much we had left of each little item; then after lots of little arithmetic problems, add up long columns correctly without a machine. It was especially complicated this month, because we had bought so much—fountain pens, lighters, and various items we had been unable to get before.

I continued to take the star sights morning and evening and sun lines during the day. I studied charts of the portion of the West Coast we were heading for. On 4 August we received a radio dispatch instructing us to change our destination from Puget Sound to Portland, Oregon.

We fueled subchasers and traded movies with them. Our men really appreciated having a movie projector on board at last.

We had basketball games again. The sea was calm, and the men wanted to get into it after forgetting about basketball for their month in port. Again we conducted drills—fire and rescue, fire, abandon ship, fire and rescue again, man overboard drill.

We learned of the atomic bomb—about our dropping the first bomb on Hiroshima on 6 August and the second on Nagasaki on 9 August. To us this was great news. We felt that this practically assured bringing the war to a prompt end—without conducting an amphibious campaign against the Japanese homeland at the cost of hundreds of thousands of American and Japanese lives.

The excitement on board heightened. Each day we were that much closer to the mainland. We looked forward to our leaves. More important, we began to focus on the likelihood that the war itself would end. The armistice proposals we heard were almost too good to believe.

For months in the Pacific, we had thought wistfully of the "Golden Gate in Forty-Eight" as the best we could hope for. It was hard to believe how much progress had been made just since we came on the scene at Leyte in October 1944!

Events were happening so fast—the atomic bombs, Soviet Russia entering the war, the President's speech, followed by the Japanese statement and our reply.

We had a celebration on Monday—a going-home party! It started with a basketball game on the tank deck. Then a buffet supper on the tank deck with fried chicken, ham, cold cuts, Coca-Cola, potato salad, olives, pickles. Cave decorated a big layer cake for the occasion. He depicted a baseball field with Leyte, Lingayen, and Okinawa on first, second, and third base and guess what on home plate?

A basketball team: front Polarevic (with ball), Lt. (jg) Montgomery, Grefost; rear: Brown, Shilling, Shiner, Bunte.

Deck division hoses down main deck for Portland arrival—Gossett, Fouty, Adams, Harrison, Baumunk, Nickles, Frederick, Houtchings, Olson and McNulty.

We watched a movie, and after that they cut the cake. We washed it down with hot chocolate. It tasted good; the weather had become quite brisk.

Everybody was feeling great. We saw happy faces everywhere. The quartermasters posted our daily mileage on the bulletin board.

On the evening of 13 August we sighted the Tillamook Light Rock at 2125 and the Columbia Lightship at 2220. At 0500 on 14 August the river pilot came aboard, and an hour later the river tug *Henderson* came along our port side to assist in taking us up the Columbia River. All day we observed some of the most beautiful scenery in the world—and the American mainland!

By 1700 we had turned into the Willamette River, approaching Portland, Oregon, when the Captain called all officers except the Officer of the Deck to his cabin. We learned that *Japan had just approved a peace agreement.*

THE WAR WAS OVER!

It was hard to believe. We took a little time to savor it. But not too much time. We soon were passing under the bridges of downtown Portland. At 1853 we moored along the *LST 273* at the Burnside Bridge.

Liberty was immediately granted to all officers and men not on the evening's watch list. I wasted no time getting on my way.

At the Multnomah Hotel just down the street I immediately put in a call to Fran. But there was about a four-hour delay for lines to Chicago. The operator said to call back at about midnight.

We walked up the street to the center of town and discovered men kissing girls and girls kissing men everywhere you looked. People were riding 15 or 20 in a car, tooting horns and trying to force their way through streets filled with people wandering around, shouting, and kissing everybody.

Stores and bars were closed up tight. Nothing for people to do but walk miles up and down the main streets, expressing their joy any way they knew how. It was a wonderful day to return to the U.S. mainland! The happiest day since people lived normal lives at home in 1940!

The river tug *Henderson* is moored to port quarter to
assist in taking us up the Columbia River through
some of the most beautiful scenery in the world.

U. S. Army Light Tug 452, which towed us on our happy return to Portland, Oregon.

I returned to the Multnomah at midnight and called long distance. This time the operator was able to put the call through. What a thrill it was when a sleepy Fran answered the phone—at something like two-thirty in the morning, her time. Despite all the hints in my letters about buses, taxis, hotels, restaurants and beaches, she hadn't been able to let herself think I was any closer than Sydney!

She quickly adapted, however, to the idea that I would be home on leave this coming Saturday morning. It was even hard for *me* to think it possible, and yet I knew that every day, every hour, we had been getting closer and closer. It was too wonderful to believe.

It suddenly occurred to me that I had been up all night the night before, navigating our way to the mouth of the Columbia River. Perhaps a couple of hours of sleep in the morning. So when I got back to the *698* and into my bunk, I can safely say that in no more than 57 seconds I was zonked. What a happy feeling!

A couple of pals—Polarevic and Farr.

Bill Chapman, Ralph Hart, and Lou Miller.

38

One Era Ends, Another Begins

*What a great feeling! I see Fran and my son Billy. I
would be released from duty—but must return to Portland
first. Some weddings are planned. As preparations are made
for decommissioning, a new officer reports for duty*

August-October 1945—Fran met me at Chicago's Midway
Airport. What a wonderful sight she was! We couldn't do anything but
hug and gaze at each other. For 15 months we had waited for this
moment! I haven't any idea whether I introduced her to the other
officers with me or whether I even said goodbye to them. Impolite as
it sounded, we couldn't think of anything else.

Bill Eklund had lined up the tickets on Northwest Airlines, leaving
Portland on Friday and arriving at Midway at 0850 the next morning.
Ralph Hart, Bill Chapman, Bruce Montgomery, Ray Kennedy, and
Angelo Prezioso (the chief) all had reservations on the same flight.
Monty left the plane at Minneapolis. The others transferred in Chicago
to planes going to their separate destinations.

This was my first long-distance trip by plane. The flight from
Portland to Chicago was in a Douglas DC-3, which carried 21
passengers in seven rows, two passengers on the left side of the aisle,
one passenger on the right. It flew to Spokane, then to Butte, Billings,

Fargo, and Minneapolis. Then *nonstop* all the way from Minneapolis to Chicago. I had told Fran of our scheduled arrival at Midway.

After I picked up my baggage, we drove back to Wilmette—to Billy and to Fran's mother. Fran told me she had barely made it to Midway. She had driven blithely along until she discovered she was near the Museum of Science and Industry—not Midway. After a 90-degree correction and about ten more miles, she arrived about the same time as the plane.

I couldn't wait to see Billy. He was as cute as I had imagined from his pictures. But then I began to learn the whole story about him. Right from birth he had not been well. He cried and cried, continually. Practically every night Fran had had to get up several times. And now this little guy had trouble holding down his meals. The pediatrician told her to give up nursing him and prescribed a pabulum mix which had to be boiled for an hour or more each day.

She began to sit next to the bathtub when feeding him, so that when she felt him begin to upchuck, she could point him in the direction of the tub. Fran had held back on telling me the difficult time she had been having since his birth six months before. She *had* written of taking him at three months to the hospital for surgery for an inguinal hernia. That had been a necessary procedure, but it had not ended the crying.

That night I heard him when he awakened crying, and I got up to go to him. Fran realized that now another person would share in going to his side.

We arranged to have him baptized. I wore my dress whites for the first time since May 1944, after my graduation from midshipman school, when we had gone dinner dancing at the Roosevelt Hotel in New Orleans—and when we had had our last dinner together at the St. Charles.

I saw my two sisters and their families, Fran's sisters and brother and all their families. Shortly we went to Madison to see Dad and my stepmother and more relatives.

Within a week or two the Navy announced a more liberal point system for release from service. Extra points would be allowed for each month of overseas duty. I qualified.

I went up to Great Lakes to the District Security Office, where I had served as an enlisted man, to see what I could do to get out, the quicker the better. They wired my request to my ship for release from active duty, but it was approved only on condition that I return to Portland first!

I was already feeling like a civilian. It seemed so simple to let me out right then and there, and avoid all that extra transportation. *Mais c'est la guerre!*

While still on leave, I went downtown to see my former employer. Yes, they'd certainly take me back—at the same salary I was making when I left, three-and-a-half years before! I decided I'd do some looking before I accepted that.

I did go back to Portland for a week, stayed at the Multnomah, and saw all the fellows again. I promptly accounted for the inventory of sextants, chronometers, and navigational equipment—and "squared away" the ship's service account. We still had an inventory of about $350 worth of stuff to get rid of, so we had a closeout sale—"back to the bare bulkheads."

I was finally on my way home, via the Thirteenth Naval District in Seattle and the Ninth Naval District in Great Lakes. On 3 October 1945, I officially received my release. I started job interviews at advertising agencies the next day.

*   *   *

Things moved rapidly at Portland. It was official that *LST 698* would be decommissioned. Leaves were cancelled for the second group. Instead, one third of the crew was transferred for leave (if they hadn't already had it) and *reassignment.* A second third would be transferred later, and the third group would remain until the ship was decommissioned. This applied to officers and men.

Ralph Hart, Bill Chapman, and Al Toll had already made plans to be married. Al and his fiancé had set their wedding date for 6 October.

When Al learned that he, Monty, and Ek would be transferred within a week to Seattle, he wondered how this would bollix up his wedding plans. Luckily, he found a benevolent reassignment officer in Seattle who gave him an immediate four-weeks' leave and then orders to report to the Philadelphia Naval Yard!

An incongruous event occurred about this time. Al Toll told me of it. In the midst of our three-tiered reduction of officers and men to an eventual zero, an officer showed up, with all his clothing and gear, to report to duty!

He had been at Pearl Harbor when he received his orders. Since our ship was not there, he was sent to San Diego. When San Diego found out where we were, he was sent on—to Seattle. He saw our ship as he passed through Portland on the way to Seattle. When he arrived, he announced that two other officers were also assigned to our ship. I have no idea how this was resolved, but I'm sure it was not long-time employment.

LST 698 was decommissioned on 26 November 1945, at 1330 in Portland. The last item in the ship's log was:

"1330 Decommissioning ceremonies held. Commanding Officer read orders from Commandant Thirteenth Naval District, serial no. 682001, dated 23 October 1945, to decommission the vessel. Colors, jack and commission pennant were struck. Commander T. P. Kellogg, USNR, accepted the vessel for the Commandant Thirteenth Naval District. Officers and men were transferred as per attached list."

The entry was signed by L. R. Miller, Lt. (jg) USNR and was approved by G. W. Gilbert, Lieut., USN, commanding, and K. M. Saunders, Lieut. USNR, navigator.

The ship was towed to Astoria, Ore., at the mouth of the Columbia River. It was sold on 25 June 1946 to Arctic Circle Exploration, Inc., Seattle. Who knows what happened after that!

39

Reflections: the War, the Navy, the Bomb

As our wartime saga came to an end, we began to focus on our family of three of which I had been an absentee member. At last I could relieve Fran of part of the responsibility for Bill. And I would get back into the job market. So I'll merely end this story with a few reflections.

The war and the navy

My respect for America's conduct of World War II has grown as I have learned more about the problems we faced in the beginning and the ways we overcame them. The timetable for these accomplishments was phenomenal.

The development of the navy's amphibious forces illustrates a single aspect of the gigantic effort by all the armed forces and folks at home to win the war. The introduction to this book tells of the design and building from scratch of the landing ship tank (LST), which did not even exist at the start of the war. With only a few minor changes, that design was used in building 1,051 LSTs by the end of the war.

The new type of amphibian operations combined the massive participation of hundreds of ships—the fast carrier groups, bombardment by ships and planes, minesweeping, underwater demolition of obstructions, and the newly created amphibious ships and craft that made it so much easier to transfer personnel, munitions, and supplies between water and land. All these forces operated on longer supply lines than ever before in history. Our *LST 698* was a vital element in a tremendous machine.

The broad planning ranged from strategies to equipment to delivery and implementation. Production time and delivery time were continually shortened as the war progressed.

To make that machine run, the navy had developed a huge personnel and education program. They selected thousands of the right men, put them in the right jobs, educated them to run all those ships, and made each ship a complete, self-sufficient entity. This was accomplished largely with the men brought into the navy after the beginning of the war—*landlubbers* from the farms and cities of America.

The bomb

Those of us who were in the Pacific at the time were excited with the news of the dropping of atomic bombs on Hiroshima and Nagasaki. With that single bomb dropped on Hiroshima on 6 August 1945, Historian Morison reports, "an estimated 71,379 people, including the military, were killed, 19,691 were seriously wounded, and about 171,000 rendered homeless."[1] This could certainly be called the greatest man-made disaster in history—the single most destructive act ever inflicted.

It was a tremendous event strategically, pragmatically, and yes, *morally*. There was no question but that the war would end much earlier than any of us had dreamed and that hundreds of thousands of lives, both American and Japanese, were *saved* by this action.

This conclusion may surprise many present-day critics of the bomb, but strong logic supports it.

The reason our ship was not repaired promptly in the spring and summer of 1945 was that the advanced base sectional docks in the

Pacific were needed by so many ships due to damage from kamikazes. Many of these ships could be returned to duty in a week or less, while our ship would have taken considerably longer. The navy was anxious to get as many ships as possible back on the line in preparation for the big one—the assault on the Japanese homeland.

Background for the proposed assault against the Japanese mainland is found in chapter 40 of *Battle Report: Victory in the Pacific,* by Capt. Walter Karig, USNR, and his colleagues, Lt. Cdr. Russell L. Harris, USNR, and Lt. Cdr. Frank A. Manson, USN. The title of the eight-page chapter is "What Might Have Been."

> On May 25 . . . the die was cast. The Joint Chiefs of Staff ordered the invasion of southern Kyushu with a target date of November 1 . . .
>
> The invasion of Kyushu was to be the biggest offensive operation yet attempted in the Pacific War, so big in fact that all the military and naval resources of the two Pacific theaters would have to be used . . . [2]

According to Karig *et al.,* two distinct fleets would be used simultaneously—the Third Fleet under Halsey, with its fast carrier groups, to provide strategic cover through air attacks on Honshu and Hokkaido, and the Fifth Fleet, under Spruance, to provide amphibious, support, and local covering forces. "As an illustration of the vastness of the operation, 210 attack transports and 555 LSTs were to be used, and they were only part of the fleet."[3]

That final battle for the homeland of Japan would have been an unimaginably bitter one. The Japanese would have fought to the last man to defend their native land. America would ultimately have won, because our forces had already nearly eliminated Japanese air power and sea power. Our bombers would have continued to hit aircraft plants, oil storage tanks, and other targets. The B-29s had already begun bombing Japan's cities. Some 500,000 had been killed by such attacks, according to one estimate.[4]

Once we committed our forces to the landings on Japan, the casualties could easily have numbered in the hundreds of thousands for each side. Much of what had been the beauty of Japan would have been destroyed.

Nobody wanted that. How much destruction would the emperor and military have accepted before they surrendered? Probably a great amount.

By dropping the bomb, America gave Japan a clear idea of what was to come. Suddenly the answer for Japan was easy. The only way to preserve what was left was to surrender. The sooner the better.

Admittedly, this is a special case, since the number of lives saved was unquestionably much greater than the number lost by the two atomic explosions.

It is doubtful that such conditions would ever exist again for justifying the bomb's use. However, by our detonating the two bombs at Hiroshima and Nagasaki, the world became fully aware of the awfulness of the bomb's powers of destruction. And this in itself became a mighty deterrent to its use.

Our family and me

I have always been thankful I came back from the war unharmed in mind and body. Fran and I were fully aware that I might not have been so fortunate. The realization that thousands died but I survived gave me great humility—and a desire to lead a life I could be proud of.

With great joy we celebrated our 50th wedding anniversary in October 1992 with our three sons, our daughter, their spouses, our six grandchildren, and many of our friends. Ten years later, in 2002, we celebrated more quietly 60 wonderful years together.

We are grateful indeed that we have been witnesses to the exciting decades that followed, and participants in it.

Notes

[1] Morison, Samuel Eliot: *History of United States Naval Operations in World War II, Volume XIV, Victory in the Pacific, 1975,* Little, Brown and Company, New York, 1945, 344-45. (Morison's footnote quoted Craven & Cate V 717, 722-

725. He added, "This seems, however, to have been an overestimate. A Japanese official notice of 31 July 1959 stated that the total number of deaths attributed to the bombing of Hiroshima, including all that had occurred in the nearly 24 years since it happened, was 60,175.")

2   Karig, Capt. Walter, USNR, Lt. Cdr. Russell L. Harris, USNR, and Lt. Cdr. Frank A. Manson, USN: *Battle Report: Victory in the Pacific,* Copyright 1949 by Rinehart & Company, Inc., New York, 455-6. Reprinted by permission of Henry Holt & Co., LLC

3   *Ibid.,* 456

4   *The Times Atlas of the Second World War,* John Keegan editor, Harper & Row Publishers, New York, 1989, 204

Where to See an LST

Over the past half century, the thousand LSTs have "dwindled down to a precious few." Some are still in use in maritime countries like Greece. But now, at last, two of these strange ships are on display for all to see: one in Mobile, Ala., the other in Muskegon, Mich.

LST 325, in Mobile, was brought across the Atlantic from Greece under Captain Bob Jornlin for display at the USS LST Ship Memorial. This ship was a veteran of three years of naval service in the European theater, including D-Day and some 50 trips from England to the French coast, earning two stars. She served in the Arctic during the '50s and then in the Greek Navy.

When the ship arrived in Mobile, she tied up at a new dock in Chickisaw, Ala., just north of Mobile. Here she went through major rebuilding and refurbishing and is now receiving crowds of tourists.

In 2003 the ship toured the lower Mississippi and Ohio Rivers, covering some 3,200 miles. She departed from Mobile on 3 June and cruised to Vicksburg and Greenville, Miss., Memphis, Tenn., Cape Girardeau and St. Louis, Mo., Evansville and Jeffersonville, Ind., Paducah, Ky., and New Orleans, La., returning to Mobile on 19 August.

Crowds toured the ship at every port—a total of more than 70,000 visitors. One high point came at Evansville, home of the shipyard where 167 LSTs had been built during World War II. In 11 days in Evansville, some 25,000 visitors came aboard. Many had helped to build the LSTs. Others had sailed on an LST during the war.

The success of this tour suggested planning another, to the East Coast, scheduled now for the summer of 2005. It will sail to Washington,

D.C., Boston, and other ports to celebrate the 60th anniversary of World War II. It will eventually sail again to Evansville, which will then become its home port. Until then the ship's address is Hooks Terminal, off U.S. Route 43, Chickasaw, Ala. Email: www.LSTmemorial.org. Telephone: 251-452-3255.

*　　*　　*

LST 393, in Muskegon, received three battle stars in WWII for meritorious action in the European campaigns of Anzio, Sicily, and D-Day.

After WWII, Sand Products Company, of Detroit, converted it into a cross-lake car carrier, operating on the Great Lakes from 1947 to 1972. It was then called the *Highway 16*. After that, it was inactive for 28 years until the year 2000.

It is now docked near the heart of downtown Muskegon, Mich. on Muskegon Lake at the West Michigan Dock & Market Corporation. Over the past three years it has been partially restored with the aid of veterans and local volunteers and is now open to visitors.

Further information can be obtained from Pat Harker at the Mart Dock, 560 Mart Street, Muskegon, MI 49440. Telephone: 231-722-4730.

LST Associations

The United States LST Association, based in Toledo, Ohio, was started in 1985. Its purpose is to get old shipmates back together and renew old friendships. It currently has about 9,800 members. Its publication, Scuttlebutt, is published bimonthly. Milan Gunjak of Oregon, Ohio, is president. The address of the association is P.O. Box 167438, Oregon, OH 43616-7438 or e-mail: uslst@kmbs.com. Telephone: 1-800-228-5870.

State LST associations have been organized in these states: Arizona, California, The Carolinas, Colorado, Connecticut, Florida, Illinois, Indiana, Iowa, Kansas, Louisiana, Massachusetts, Michigan, Minnesota, Nevada, New Hampshire, New York, Ohio, Oregon, Pennsylvania, Tennessee, Texas, Washington, Wisconsin, and West Virginia.

LST Shipyard Museum

The Evansville Museum of Arts, History and Science in Evansville, Ind., has a 7-foot architectural model of a 542-class LST and a virtual museum containing LST memorabilia. These include plan drawings of the LST and 40 images of the historic shipyard, showing LSTs in various stages of construction.

The museum is located at 411 S.E. Riverside Drive in Evansville. Tom Lonnberg is the curator of history. Telephone: 812-425-2406. The website is www.emuseum.org.

Where the LSTs Were Built

The need was great, from the start of World War II, to produce LSTs and other amphibious craft as rapidly as possible. But all the coastal shipbuilders were already up to their ears turning out conventional ships—the destroyers, carriers, transports. So plants were created along the inland waterways, and new mass production techniques were developed to turn out these massive ships in record time. A total of 1,051 LSTs were produced,

Together these five plants, along the Ohio and the Illinois Rivers, turned out some 700 of these ships: American Bridge, Ambridge, Pa.; Chicago Bridge and Iron, Seneca, Ill.; Dravo Corp., Pittsburgh, Pa.; Jeffersonville Boat and Machine, Jeffersonville, Ind.; and Missouri Valley Bridge and Iron, Evansville, Ind. The last of these was the leader in total output, producing 167 LSTs.

The remainder were built by these seaboard shipyards: Bethlehem-Fairfield, Baltimore, Md.; Bethlehem-Hingham, Hingham, Mass.; Bethlehem Steel, Quincy., Mass.; Boston Navy Yard, Boston, Mass.; Charleston Navy Yard, Charleston, S. C.; Dravo Corp., Wilmington, Del.; Kaiser, Inc., Vancouver, Wash.; Kaiser, Inc., Richmond, Calif.; Newport News Shipyard, Newport News, Va.; Norfolk Navy Yard, Norfolk, Va.; and Philadelphia Navy Yard, Philadelphia, Pa.

Itinerary—U.S.S. LST 698, 1944-1945

From	To		Nautical Miles
3-Jun-44		Ship commissioned, New Orleans, La.	
3-Jun	9-Jun	Ship retrofitting, New Orleans, La.	
9-Jun	10-Jun	Underway, New Orleans, La., to St. Andrews Bay, Panama City, Fla.	304
11-Jun	24-Jun	Undergoing shakedown, Panama City, Fla.	
24-Jun	26-Jun	Underway, Panama City, Fla., to Gulfport, Miss.	202
26-Jun	28-Jun	Loading Quonset huts, Gulfport, Miss.	
28-Jun	29-Jun	Underway, Gulfport, Miss., to New Orleans, La.	207
29-Jun	8-Jul	Additional retrofitting at New Orleans; loaded LCT onto main deck	
8-Jul	14-Jul	Underway, New Orleans, La., to Guantantamo Bay, Cuba	958
15-Jul	18-Jul	At Guantanamo Bay, Cuba	
18-Jul	22-Jul	Underway, Guantanamo Bay to Coco Solo, Panama Canal Zone	684

24-Jul	24-Jul	Passing through Panama Canal	
24-Jul	7-Aug	Underway, Coco Solo to San Diego, Calif.	2,828
7-Aug	11-Aug	Loading additional supplies, San Diego	
11-Aug	22-Aug	Underway, San Diego to Pearl Harbor, Oahu, Territory of Hawaii	2,224
22-Aug	31-Aug	At Pearl Harbor	
1-Sep	2-Sep	Underway, Pearl Harbor to Maui, T.H.	42
3-Sep	3-Sep	Exercises off Maui	
4-Sep	5-Sep	Underway, Maui to Pearl Harbor	42
5-Sep	7-Sep	At Pearl Harbor	
7-Sep	8-Sep	Underway, Pearl Harbor to Kaneohe Bay	13
9-Sep	10-Sep	Loaded troops and vehicles	
10-Sep	25-Sep	Underway, Oahu to Eniwetok Atoll, Marshall Islands	2,354
25-Sep	26-Sep	Loaded provisions at Eniwetok	
26-Sep	4-Oct	Underway, Eniwetok to Manus, Admiralty Islands	1,185
5-Oct	11-Oct	Loaded supplies at Seeadler Harbor, Manus	
12-Oct	20-Oct	Underway, Manus to Leyte, Philippine Islands	1,531
20-Oct	24-Oct	At Dulag, Leyte, unloaded troops in third wave of invasion; LCVPs carried supplies to beach; LCT launched from main deck	
24-Oct	30-Oct	Underway, Leyte to Hollandia, Dutch New Guinea, Netherlands East Indies	1,226
31-Oct	4-Nov	At Humboldt Bay, Hollandia	

5-Nov	6-Nov	Underway, Hollandia to Biak, Schouten Islands, Netherlands East Indies	298
7-Nov	8-Nov	At Biak	
9-Nov	9-Nov	Loaded troops, vehicles at Mios Woendi, Schouten Islands, N.E.I.	
9-Nov	15-Nov	Underway, Biak to Leyte, Philippine Islands	961
15-Nov	16-Nov	Unloaded troops and equipment at Leyte	
16-Nov	22-Nov	Underway, Leyte to Hollandia, Dutch New Guinea, N.E.I.	1,231
22-Nov	3-Dec	At Humboldt Bay, Hollandia	
4-Dec	8-Dec	Underway, Hollandia to Finschhafen, Papua New Guinea	500
8-Dec	11-Dec	Loaded medical unit at Finschhafen	
11-Dec	18-Dec	Underway, Finschhafen to Morotai, Netherlands East Indies	1,280
18-Dec	1-Jan-45	Unloaded medical unit at Morotai; loaded army engineer troops and equipment	
1-Jan	11-Jan	Underway, Morotai to Lingayen Gulf, Luzon, Philippine Islands	1,346
11-Jan	19-Jan	Unloaded troops and equipment over causeways to beach at Lingayen Gulf	
19-Jan	23-Jan	Underway, Lingayen Gulf to Tacloban, Leyte, Philippine Islands	770
23-Jan	30-Jan	At Tacloban	
30-Jan	9-Feb	Underway, Tacloban to Manus, Admiralty Islands	1,536

9-Feb	23-Feb	Loaded supplies at Seeadler Harbor, Manus; starboard bulkhead repaired at advanced base sectional dock	
23-Feb	1-Mar	Underway, Manus to Port Purvis, Florida Island, Solomon Islands	1,027
1-Mar	15-Mar	At Florida and Guadalcanal Islands, Solomon Islands; loaded Seabee troops, vehicles, equipment, explosives	
15-Mar	24-Mar	Underway, Port Purvis, Florida Island to Ulithi Atoll, West Caroline Islands	1,721
24-Mar	27-Mar	Loaded additional provisions at Ulithi	
27-Mar	2-Apr	Underway, Ulithi to Okinawa, Ryukyu Islands	1,195
2-Apr	4-Apr	At Kerama Retto, Okinawa Gunto	
4-Apr	8-Apr	Underway to Okinawa Jima; unloaded Seabee troops, vehicles, equipment, explosives; damaged the ship on outlying coral reef	
8-Apr	8-Apr	Towed to Kerama Retto	
8-Apr	14-Apr	At Kerama Retto	
14-Apr	23-Apr	Towed from Kerama Retto to Ulithi Atoll, West Caroline Islands	1,195
23-Apr	19-May	At Ulithi	
19-May	4-Jun	Towed from Ulithi to Eniwetok Atoll, Marshall Islands	1,349
4-Jun	7-Jun	At Eniwetok; rerigged towline	

7-Jun	26-Jun	Towed from Eniwetok to Pearl Harbor, Oahu, Territory of Hawaii	2,312
26-Jun	30-Jul	Awaited repair order at Pearl Harbor	
30-Jul	14-Aug	Towed from Pearl Harbor to Portland, Ore.	2,334
14-Aug	26-Nov	Moored at Portland; began closedown of ship and transfer of personnel	
26-Nov		Ship decommissioned, Portland	
		Total nautical miles	*32,855*

Passengers and

Cargo Carried

This list is incomplete but gives an indication of the work done by a single LST in World War II. The total was undoubtedly exceeded by many LSTs which were in service longer or made shorter, more frequent runs. LST 698 also supplied water and fuel to smaller ships.

Dates	Origin/ Destination	Passengers	Cargo
24 Jun 44/ Aug 44	Gulfport, Miss.,/Pearl Harbor, T.H.		Prefabricated Quonset huts
30 Jun 44/ 20 Oct 44	New Orleans, La./ Leyte, Philippines	1 officer, 12 men for LCT 898	LCT 898 hoisted onto main deck
2 Sep 44 5 Sep 44	Koko Head, Oahu, T.H./ Keawakapu & Maalaea, Maui, T.H./ Pearl Harbor, T.H.	17 officers, 269 men, U. S. Army Infantry + 1 officer, 12 men for LCT 898	LVTs & DUKWs (amphibious tanks) for practice exercises
7 Sep 44/ 20 Oct 44	Pearl Harbor, T.H./Leyte, Philippines	As above, + 2 officers, 103 men	
10 Sep 44/ 20 Oct 44	Kaneohe Bay & Maunalua Bay, T.H./Leyte, Philippines	As above	LVTs & DUKWs

7 Nov 44/ 15 Nov 44	Biak Is., Schouten Is., Netherlands East Indies/Leyte, Philippines	29 officers, 255 men	Vehicles & equipment
10 Dec 44/ 18 Dec 45	Finschafen, New Guinea/ Morotai, Netherlands East Indies	19 officers, 262 men of 108 Medical Battalion, 33rd Infantry Division	Vehicles, equipment, including white ambulances on main deck
31 Dec 44/ 17 Jan 45	Morotai, N.E.I./ Lingayen, Luzon, Philippines	8 officers, 185 men of 6th Army engineering unit	Bulldozers, graders, other road building equipment, Bailey bridges
5 Mar 45/ 7 Apr 45	Florida Is., Solomon Is./ Ulithi, West Carolines/ Okinawa, Ryukyu Is.	11 officers, 142 men of 4th USN CB regiment & USN CB battalion	Construction vehicles & equipment, TNT, 100 octane gasoline
19 May 45/ 27 Jun 45	Ulithi, West Carolines/Pearl Harbor, Oahu, T. H.	8 officers, 100 men of disabled LST 884	

Shipmates : The Men Who Ran the *LST 698*

They Came from 37 of the 48 States

(Roster compiled from various sources. Ranks and rates are those at start of cruise. Nicknames in parentheses are often used in text for brevity.)

The officers:

GILBERT, Lt. Glen W. (the captain or skipper), Grayson, La., commanding officer

SAUNDERS, Lt. (jg) Kenneth M. (Sandy), Oakmont, Pa., executive officer

CHAPMAN, Ens. Judson W. (Bill or Ben), Greenville, S.C., communication officer

CRITES, Ens. Robert (Bob), Indianapolis, Ind., boat officer with six men on temporary duty from Hollandia to Pearl Harbor

EKLUND, Ens. William A. (Ek), Austin, Texas, first lieutenant

ERICKSON, Lt. (jg) Edwin M. (Eric), Moorhead, Minn., supply officer

HART, Ens. Ralph V. (Ralph), St. Louis, Mo., assistant first lieutenant

HASWELL, Ens. Homer A. (Homer), Wilmette, Ill., assistant navigator, the author

KENNEDY, Ens. Raymond J. (Ray), Oakville, Conn., gunnery officer

MILLER, Ens. Louis (Lou), Burlingame, Calif., boat officer

MONTGOMERY, Ens. Bruce (Bruce), South Minneapolis, Minn., boat officer

PREZIOSO, Lt. (jg) Angelo H. (the chief), Youngstown, Ohio, engineering officer

TOLL, Ens. Albert C. (Al), Philadelphia, Pa., assistant first lieutenant

Enlisted men (incomplete):

ACORD, Bill Hugh, F1c (MoMM), Bisbee, Ariz.

ADAMS, Carlos Jr., S2c, Dayton, Ohio

ALDRIDGE, James B., S2c, Winfield, Ala.

ALEXANDER, Richard B., S2c, Calvert City, Ky., gyrocompass

ALFONSO, Italo, S2c, Coal City, Pa.

ANDERSON, Donald E., S2c, Galva, Ill.

ANTICH, Paul J., S2c, Detroit, Mich.

ARUSSELL, Elden, MoMM2c, Roberson, N.D.

BARBER, Robert B., SC1c, Searcy, Ark., head cook, butcher

BARK, Myron C., SC1 (GM), Tarentum, Pa., gunner's mate, mailman

BAUMONK, Burgess R., S2c, Findley, Ohio

BAVOUSETT, Glenn B. (Tex), S2c (RdM), Fort Worth, Texas, radarman

BAZEMORE, Luther E. H., S1c, Baltimore, Md.

BEACH, James T., SF3c, Baltimore, Md., shipfitter

BENNETT, James P., S2c (SK), Miami, Fla.

BENSON, William H., SF3c, New York, N. Y., coxswain

BIHN, Kenneth L., S2c, Dayton, Ohio

BLAKENEY, Rex B., F2c (EM), Spruce Pine, N. C.

BOUCHER, Normand R, F2c (EM), Nashua, N. H.

BOYER, Willard D., F2c, W. Tooele, Utah

BROWN, Clifford T., GM3c, W. Warwick, R.I.

BROWN, Courtney E., F2c

BRUMMITT, C. L., F1c (MoMM), Quincy, Mass.

BUNTEN, L. R., Sioux City, Iowa

BURGESS, James R., S1c(SM), Arlington, Va.

CALHOUN, Harold L., F2c, Vernonia, Ore.

CAVE, Arthur J., SC2c, Bismarck, N.D., cook, worship leader

CLARKE, John J., S2c, Bronx, N. Y.

CLINGEN, Alton L., QM3c, Orange, N.J., quartermaster

COLEMAN, Robert F., PhM3c, Roxbury, Mass.

COLLINS, William J., F2c, Bronx, N. Y.

CORMIER, H. J., MoMM3c, Littleton, Mass.

CORRIS, Charles E., S1c, Devon, Conn.

COSTA, Jack, S1c, Bristol, R. I.

COSTELLA, Philip J., S2c, Santa Cruz, Calif.

COTE, Roland Leo, S2c (Bkr), Manchester, N.H., baker

COX, James S., S2c, Mingus, Texas

CREAN, Robert E., S2c, Catawissa, Mo.

D'ANGELO, Thomas J., S2c (BM), Easton, Pa.

DE FILLIPPO, Michael, S1c, Willimantic, Conn.

DE HAAN, Walter, F2c

DEMENT, G. A. Indianapolis, Ind.

DENNIS, W. T., StM2c, Clarkston, Ga.

DOMINIAK, Casimir, S2c (BM), South Bend, Ind.

DUTCH, Francis J., SK3c, Monongahela, Pa., storekeeper

FARR, Francis R., S1c (FC), Philadelphia, Pa.

FLOWERS, Marlin O., S2c

FOUTY, Charles W., S2c, Glovers Gap, W. Va.

FREDERICK, Lawrence, S2c, Detroit, Mich.

GALLIHER, McClellan T., S2c, Elizabethton, Tenn.

GAUTHIER, Richard G., S2c, Newark, N.J.

GEE, Morris R. S2c, Bedford, Ind.

GENTRY, Paul F., S2c, Shelbyville, Tenn., cook

GIOVANNIELLO, William, F1c (MoMM), Elmhurst, N. Y.

GOFF, Allen T., S2c, Danville, Ill.

GONZALEZ, Orlando, S1c(RM), Brooklyn, N. Y.

GORMLEY, James J., S1c, Philadelphia, Pa.

GOSSETT, Isaac W., S2c, Steubenville, Ohio

GRAY, Joseph R., S2c, Ava, Ill.

GREEN, Vernon H. (Stubby), SF3c, Bellevue, Ohio, shipfitter

GREFOST, Robert J., GM3c, Elizabeth, Pa.

GROMAN, William H., S2c, Bethlehem, Pa.

HAHN, John J., S2c, Mosinee, Wis.

HAMILTON, Wesley B., S2c (RM), Charleston, S. C.

HANCOCK, Robert J., S2c, Skowhegan, Maine

HANNON, Richard M., S1c (SM), signalman

HARRINGTON, Paul E., S2c, Chillicothe, Ohio

HARRISON, Charlie W. (Popeye), S2c, Colfax, W.Va.

HEALY, Paul S., MoMM2c, Roslindale, Mass.

HENSLE, George F., S2c, Chicago, Ill.

HENTHORN, Ivan D. (Doc), PhM2c, Porter Falls, W.Va., pharm. mate

HEPNER, Max B., SC3c, New York, N.Y., cook

HICKE, W. M., LaCrosse, Wis.

HICKMAN, George T., StM2c, Marion Station, Md., steward's mate

HILL, Wayne H., S2c, Northfield, Vt.

HOCKIN, Wynn D., F2c, Flint, Mich.

HOUTCHINGS, Leon B., S2c, Randleman, N. C.

KING, William J., SM2c, Madison, Wis.

KING, James J., BM1c, Birmingham, Ala.

KINNISON, Richard L., PhM2c, Alden, Mich.

KORTE, Bernard H., Jr., F2c, St. Louis, Mo.

LAWING, Jack S., Sr., F1c (MoMM), Cramenton, N. C.

LEWIS, Dean M., F1c (MoMM), Fayville, Mass.

LOARD, Milton W., sS2c, Montgomery, Ala

MACLAREN, J. R., F2c, Port Huron, Mich.

MAJID, Kemal A., S1c (GM), Brooklyn, N.Y., radio technician

MAJKRZAK, Stanley A., F1c, Cleveland, Ohio

MARGICIN, Andrew A., MoMM3c, Trenton, N. J.

MARTIN, Lynn W, Y2c, Houston, Mo., yeoman

MC CLINTON, Oscar R., S2c, McCalla, Ala.

MC CONNELL, Rufus P., S2c, Mobile, Ala.

MC GUIRE, William M., S2c, North Braddock, Pa.

MC NULTY, William J., S2c, Hazleton, Pa.

MELANSON, Leo J., S2c, Rumford, Maine

MILES, Joseph D., Jr., S1c, South Norfolk, Va.

MOSS, William T., S1c, Norfolk, Va.

MYERS, Robert C., S2c, Magnolia, W. Va.

MYRICKS, George, StM2c, Birmingham, Ala.

NEWBERRY, Glen E., S2c, Auburn, Ill.

NICHOLS, I. E., BM1c, Anaheim, Calif.

NIDA, Richard B., S2c, Rand, W. Va.

NIMMO, C. L., Ona, W. Va.

OGDEN, Joe, S2c, Liberty, Miss.

OLSON, Arne, S2c, Adams, Minn.

O'NEIL, James A., S2c, Columbus, Ohio

POLAREVIC, Alexander N., GM3c, Chicago, Ill., gunner's mate, dancer

POOLE, Charles L., Jr., S2c, Durham, N. C.

POSTON, Buford, S1c, Donalsonville, Ga.

PRINCIPE, J. J., S2c

RAND, Stuart L., S2c, Everett, Mass.

RATCLIFF, Winnsboro, La.

RAY, Edward J., EM3c, Sutton, W. Va.

ROBBINS, John L. F1c (MM), Cherry Valley, Ill.

ROBERTSON, George W., F1c (MM)

ROLOW, Willard J., MoMM3c, Turner, Ore., motor machinist

RUSHING, A. C., S2c

SCHAFFER, Edward M., F1c (MoMM), Lorain, Ohio

SCHOEN, Charles A. Jr., F1c, (MoMM) (the mole), Ozone Park, N.Y.

SCHUTTE, R. H., Chicago, Ill.

SHILLING, Cecil D. S2c (GM), Pico, Calif.

SHINER, Joseph S., S2c (GM), Bethlehem, Pa.

SIDES, Eldon F., S2c, Bartley, Neb.

SILL, George F., F1c (MoMM), Mt. Oliver, Pa.

SMITH, Ernest T., BM2c, Plantersville, Ala.

SMITH, Ralph E., S1c (QM), Catlett, Va.

SOFIELD, Charles E., EM3c, Perth Amboy, N.J., electrician, refrigeration

SPENCER, Rodney B., S2c, Madison, Wis.

SPILLBERG, Arthur, MoMM2c, Iowa City, Iowa

SULLIVAN, John L., S2c, Buffalo, N. Y.

TAGLANG, Roy, MoMM3c, Jersey City, N. J.

TOPOLYAN, Stephan, S2c, Duquesne, Pa.

TOUPIN, Jean A., S2c, Fall River, Mass.

VOUDRY, Lee T., SC3c, Gloversville, N.Y., cook
WAGNER, S., Dumas, Ark.
WESTERMANN, Karl H., F2c, Franklin Square, N. Y.
WHITE, Thomas J., coxswain
WINSOR, Edward F., S2c, Moosup, Conn., signalman
ZIMMERMAN, Clarence F., Jr., S1c, Bridgeton, N. J.

LCT 898:

(On board *LST 698* from New Orleans to Leyte)

NEUMAN, L., Ensign; BAXTER, W. J., F1c; BUDD, C. W., F1c; CULLEN, T. M., S2c; ELLIOTT, R. C., S1c; GLOVER, J. C., S2c; HALL, C. J., S1c; HAMMONDS, J. R., S2c; HURLEY, J. P., F1c; KINSER, R. J., S2c; PAYNE, B. S., S1c; SLY, T. J., S1c; TRUTTMAN, L. H., F1c.

LCS 22:

(On board *LST 698* from Hollandia to Pearl Harbor)

CRITES, Robert J., D-V(G), Ensign; RATCLIFF, R. J., Cox.; SHEROKY, E. C., F1c; SHIVERS, E. B., Cox.; VELEZ, M. J., S1c; WADE, Homer "U" "L", S1c; WAGNER, Sidney (n), S1c.

Report of Damage to

U.S.S. LST 698

From Commanding Officer, LST 698 to
Commander in Chief, U. S. Fleet

7 April 1945

1. Damage suffered by this vessel during unloading operations while beached on Green beach, western coast Okinawa Jima, Nansei Shoto, Ryukyu Islands, was as follows:

2. Machinery damage listed in paragraph (3) was caused by action of heavy surf and settling during low tide onto coral reef and adjacent coral heads while beached April 5, 1945. Structural and shell damage listed in paragraph (4) was caused by pontoon causeway holding clips on LSTs 767 and 798, beached close aboard on either side, pounding into sides of ship under action of heavy surf while beached without use of disabled engines April 7, 1945.

3. (1) Machinery damage:

    (a) Main engine automatic propulsion control box warped.

    (b) Fire and flushing pump, main engine room, out of alignment.

(c) After three strut bearings on port main shaft out of alignment, shaft sprung.

(d)   After three strut bearings on starboard main shaft out of alignment, shaft sprung.

(e) Port main engine bed plate sprung; engine out of alignment; lube oil filter sprung.

(f) Starboard main engine bed plate sprung; engine out of alignment; lube oil lines to filters, pump and coolers sprung and/or broken; lube oil filter sprung.

4. (1) Frame members and shell plates:

(a) Amidships longitudinal keel member bent upwards between frames 31 and 35. Athwartships members under main engines bent upwards and deck plates sprung same location.

(b) Amidships longitudinal keel member and athwartships frame members bent upwards, frame 39. Bottom shell plates buckled.

(c) Tanks A-401-V and A-402-V taking water slowly.

(d)   Compartments C-204-L and C-202-L, shell plates, longitudinal and vertical frame members badly buckled.

(e) Third deck compartments, port and starboard sides, between frames 41 and 10, shell plates buckled, longitudinal and vertical frame members buckled, no breaks through shell.

(f) Port and starboard shaft alley bottom longitudinal frame members buckled.

(g) Main deck plates buckled starboard side, between frames 13 and 38.

(h)   Trackways number one and six boat davits buckled.

G. W. GILBERT

Information Sources

1. Itinerary for *U.S.S. LST 698*—11 June 1944 to14 August 1945, prepared by ship's yeoman
2. United States LST Association roster of *LST 698* enlisted men and officers, dated 1 November 1991
3. List of officers, *U.S.S. LST 698,* dated 2 December 1944

Ships' logs

4. Deck log remarks sheets for *U.S.S. LST 698*
   3 June to 8 July 1944
   1 to 10 September 1944
   26 September 1944
   12 to 24 October 1944
   31 October to 4 November 1944
   7 to 16 November 1944
   22 November 1944 to 31 January 1945
   9 February to 27 February 1945
   1 March to 19 May 1945
   24 to 28 May 1945
   4 June 1945
   7 June 1945
   15 to 16 June 1945
   26 June 1945
   30 July 1945 to 16 August 1945
   26 November 1945

5. Deck log columnar sheets for *U.S.S. LST 698*
    4 to 9 December 1944
    26 to 29 December 1944
    18 to 20 January 1945
    24 to 29 January 1945
    2 to 7 April 1945
    10 April 1945
    26 to 30 April 1945
    24 to 25 May 1945
    15 to 16 June 1945

6. Deck log remarks sheets, *U.S.S. LST 599*
    3 to 6 April 1945

7. Deck log remarks sheets for *U.S.S. LST 701*
    18 to 20 January 1945

8. Deck log columnar sheets for *U.S.S. LST 701*
    18 to 20 January 1945

9. Deck log remarks sheets for *U.S.S. LST 884*
    1 to 6 April 1945

Navigation charts

10. CS4209, Lingayen Gulf, West Coast of Luzon, U. S. Coast & Geodetic Survey, Manila, P. I., March 1924, reissued 1941

11. CS4305, Mindoro and Vicinity, U. S. Coast & Geodetic Survey, Manila, P. I., 1939

12. CS4423, Southern Part of Samar and San Pedro Bay, U. S. Coast & Geodetic Survey, Manila, P. I., 1938, reissued July 1940

13. CS4719, Surigao Strait and Leyte, U. S. Coast & Geodetic Survey, Manila, P.I. 1936, reissued 1941

14. HO2338, Okinawa Gunto, U. S. Hydrographic Office, 4th edition, December 1932

15. HO2985, Admiralty Islands, Manus Island, Adjacent Islands, U. S. Hydrographic Office, 1943
16. HO5202, Caroline Islands, Approaches to Palau Islands, U. S. Hydrographic Office, 1938
17. HO5205, Okinawa Jima, Southern Part, U. S. Hydrographic Office, September 1944
18. HO5413, Marshall Islands, Northern Portion, U. S. Hydrographic Office, 1923
19. HO5590, Pacific Ocean, Western Part, U. S. Hydrographic Office, October 1931
20. HO5805, Philippine Sea, U. S. Hydrographic Office, October 1931

Action reports

21. Action Report, Commander LST Flotilla 3, Assault and Occupation of Leyte, Philippine Islands, dated 7 November 1944 (covers landings on San Jose, Leyte from 20 to 24 October 1944)
22. Action Report, *U.S.S. LST 698,* Attack on Philippine Islands, dated 31 October 1944 (includes chronological account of action 20 to 24 October)
23. Action Report, Commander Task Group 79.5 (Commander LST Flotilla 6), Lingayen Gulf Operation (CTG 79.5), Serial 021, dated 11 February 1945 (covers landing units of 37th Infantry Division east of Lingayen from 9 to 18 January 1945)
24. War Diary, Commander LST Flotilla 6 (11 to 31 January 1945), dated 1 February 1945 for Task Unit 78.11.8 (formed as a returning echelon from Lingayen Gulf, Luzon, P. I., to Leyte)
25. Action Report, Commander Task Group 53.7, Commander LST Flotilla 23, Serial 042, dated 18 April 1945. Occupation of Okinawa Jima, Nansei Shoto, (covers landing support units and equipment—Marine—north of Hagushi in western Okinawa from 2 to 17 April 1945)
26. Ship's Action Report, *USS LST 698,* serial 003-45, dated 7 April 1945 (report of operational damage sustained from pounding

by other LSTs while beached on Green Beach, Okinawa; in Task Force 53.7 as part of Northern Defense Group, 5 April 1945)

27. Ship's Action Report, *USS LST 698,* serial 003-45, dated 14 April 1945, (covers unloading personnel and equipment on western Okinawa on 2 to 14 April 1945)

28. Anti-Aircraft Action Report, *U.S.S. LST 599,* dated 9 April 1945

29. Anti-Aircraft Action Report, *U.S.S. LST 884,* dated 27 April 1945

30. Ship's Damage Report, *U.S.S. LST 884,* 13 May 1945

Books

31. Alexander, Joseph H.: *Storm Landings: Epic Amphibious Battles in the Central Pacific,* Naval Institute Press, Annapolis, 1997

32. American Heritage: *Pictorial Atlas of United States History,* Edited by Hilde Heun Kagan, American Heritage Publishing Co., Inc., New York

33. *American Military Casualties and Burials,* National Archives and Records Administration, 1993

34. Astor, Gerald: *Crisis in the Pacific, the Battles for the Philippine Islands by the Men Who Fought Them—an Oral History,* Donald I. Fine Books, New York, 1996

35. Barbey, Vice Admiral Daniel E.: *MacArthur's Amphibious Navy,* Naval Institute Press, Annapolis, 1969

36. Barger, Melvin D.: *Large Slow Target, Vol. II,* A History of the Landing Ships (LSTs) and the Men Who Sailed on Them, copyright 1989 by The United States LST Association, Taylor Publishing Co., Dallas, Texas

37. Commager, Henry Steel: *The Story of the Second World War,* Brassey's (US), Inc., Div. of Maxwell Macmillan, Inc., 1991; reprint, first published by Little, Brown and Company, New York, 1945

38. Dear, I. C. B., editor: *Oxford Companion to World War II,* Oxford University Press, Oxford, New York, 1995

39. Ellis, John: *World War II, a Statistical Survey,* Facts on File

40. Forrestel, E. P.: *Admiral Raymond A. Spruance, USN, A Study in Command*, Department of the Navy, Washington, 1966

41. Freuchen, Peter: *Peter Freuchen's Book of the Seven Seas*, Julius Messner, Inc., New York, 1957

42. Gailey, Harry A: *War in the Pacific, from Pearl Harbor to Tokyo Bay*, Presidio Press, Novato, CA, 1995

43. Goralski, Robert: *World War II Almanac, 1931-1945*, G. P. Putnam & Sons, New York

44. Hashiya, Michihiko, M.D.: *Hiroshima Diary*, University of North Carolina Press, 1955

45. Heiferman, Ronald: *U. S. Navy in World War II*, Hamlyn, London, New York, Sydney, Toronto

46. Hoyt, Edwin Palmer: *How They Won the War in the Pacific—Nimitz and His Admirals*, Weybrook and Talley, 1970

47. Hoyt, Edwin Palmer: *Japan's War: The Great Pacific Conflict, 1853 to 1952*, McGraw-Hill Book Co., New York, 1986

48. Iseley, Jeter Allen, and Philip A. Crowl: *The U. S. Marines and Amphibious War*, Princeton University Press, 1951

49. James, D. Clayton, Anne Sharp Wells: *From Pearl Harbor to V-J Day, American Armed Forces in World War II*, American Ways Series, Ivan R. Dee, 1975

50. Karig, Capt. Walter: *Battle Report, Vol. V, Victory in the Pacific*, Rinehart & Co., New York, 1949

51. Keegan, John: *The Second World War*, Viking Penguin, New York, London, 1990

52. McCullough, David: *The Path between the Seas, the Creation of the Panama Canal. 1870-1914*, copyright 1977 by David McCullough, Simon and Schuster, New York, 1977

53. Michel, Henri: *The Second World War*, Praeger Publishers, New York, 1975

54. Mooney, James L., editor: *Dictionary of American Naval Fighting Ships, Vol. IV*, Naval Historical Center, Washington, 1969

55. Mooney, James L., editor: *Dictionary of American Naval Fighting Ships, Vol. VII*, Naval History Division, Washington 1969

56. Morison, Samuel Eliot: *The Two-Ocean War*, Little, Brown and Company, New York, 1963

57. Morison, Samuel Eliot: *History of United States Naval Operations in World War II, Vol. V, The Struggle for Guadalcanal, August 1942-February 1943*, Little, Brown and Company, New York, 1949

58. Morison, Samuel Eliot: *History of United States Naval Operations in World War II, Vol. VII, Aleutians, Gilberts and Marshalls, June 1942-April 1944*, Little, Brown and Company, New York, 1951

59. Morison, Samuel Eliot: *History of United States Naval Operations in World War II, Vol. VIII, New Guinea and the Marianas, March 1944-August 1944*, Little, Brown and Company, New York, 1953

60. Morison, Samuel Eliot: *History of United States Naval Operations in World War II, Vol. XII, Leyte, June 1944-January 1945*, Little, Brown and Company, New York, 1958

61. Morison, Samuel Eliot: *History of United States Naval Operations in World War II, Vol. XIII, Liberation of the Philippines—Luzon, Mindanao, Visayas, 1944-45*, Little, Brown and Company, New York, 1959

62. Morison, Samuel Eliot: *History of United States Naval Operations in World War II, Vol. XIV, Victory in the Pacific, 1945*, Little, Brown and Company, New York, 1975

63. Morison, Samuel Eliot: *History of United States Naval Operrations in World War II, Vol. X, Supplement and General Index*, Little, Brown and Company, New York, 1962

64. Murray, Williamson, and Allen M. Willett: *A War to be Won: Fighting the Second World War*, Belknap Press of Harvard University Press, Cambridge, Mass., 2000

65. Newman, Robert P.: *Truman and the Hiroshima Cult*, Michigan State University Press, East Lansing, Mich., 1995

66. Nichols, Major Chas. S.,Jr.: *Okinawa: Victory in the Pacific*, U. S. Marine Corps, 1955

67. Parrish, Thomas: *Simon & Schuster Encyclopedia of World War I*, A Cord Communications Book

68. Polmar, Norman: *The Ships and Aircraft of the U. S. Fleet*, Naval Institute Press, Annapolis, Maryland

69. Polmar, Norman: *World War II, America at War, 1941-1945*, 1991

70. Prange, Gordon W.: *At Dawn We Slept, The Untold Story of Pearl Harbor*, Penguin Books, New York, 1981

71. Smith, S. E., editor: *United States Navy in World War II,* William Morrow & Co., Inc., New York, 1966

72. *Times, The: Atlas of the Second World War,* edited by John Keenan, Harper and Row, New York, 1989

73. Van der Vat: *The Pacific War, World War II, The U.S.-Japanese Naval War, 1941-1945,* A Touchstone Book, Simon & Schuster, New York, 1941

74. Wilford, John Noble: *The Mapmakers, Revised Edition,* Alfred A. Knopf, New York, 2000

75. Woodward, C. Vann: *The Battle for Leyte Gulf,* The Macmillan Compay, New York, 1947

76. Yahara, Col. Hiromichi: *The Battle for Okinawa, a Japanese Officer's Eyewitness Account of the Last Great Campaign of World War II,* copyright 1995, Pacific Basin Institute, John Wiley & Sons, Inc., New York

Periodicals

77. *LifeTimes* (BlueCross BlueShield of Illinois), "Seneca on the Illinois built LSTs in World War II," April 2003, p. 19

78. *LST Scuttlebutt* (U.S. LST Association), various issues

79. *National Geographic Magazine,* "Landing Craft for Invasion," by Melville Bell Grosvenor, July 1944

80. *Time,* 30 October 1944 (Leyte)

81. *Time,* 6 November 1944 (Leyte)

82. *Time,* 13 November 1944 (Leyte)

83. *Time,* 23 April 1945 (Okinawa)

Compact Disks

84. *Maps 'N' Facts,* Broderbund, Novato, Calif., 1994

Letters

85. Author's letters to his wife, Frances Ellis Haswell, June 1944 to September 1945

86. Recent letters to author from LST 698 officers
87. Letter to author from Alfred J. Geary, Sm2c, USCG, *LST 884*, dated 18 August 1999

Internet

The Internet has many items on LSTs. Some of them:

88. United States LST Association. http://www.uslst.org
89. What is an LST? http://www.xmission.com~jcander/definiti.htm
90. Basic LST (Information. http://www.isers.erols.com/reds1/ LST173htmfiles/LST173_LST_info.htm
91. USS LST Ship Memorial. Story of LST 325, used in Greece since World War II and brought to Mobile, Ala., to serve as an LST ship memorial. http://www.LSTmemorial.org
92. NavSource Online: Amphibious Photo Archive LST 662. Six photos. http://www.navsource,org/archives/10/160662.htm
93. An inside look: Landing Ship Tank design, beaching equipment, decks, schematic, photos. http://www.insideLST.com/ design.htm

About the Author

Though Homer Haswell has been a writer all his life, now at 87 he has written his first book.

Born in Madison, Wis., in 1917, he graduated from the University of Wisconsin in 1939, majoring in journalism. He came to Chicago to begin a career in advertising. When World War II broke out, he left his copywriter job to become a yeoman at the Navy's Ninth Naval District at Great Lakes, Ill.

Shortly after, at a U.S.O. dance in Waukegan, Ill., he danced with Frances Ellis, of Wilmette, Ill. He discovered that everything about her seemed "just right." They married in October 1942 and have now celebrated their 62nd anniversary.

In January 1944 he enrolled in midshipman school at Northwestern University's Abbott Hall in Chicago. On being commissioned in May, he received orders to proceed to New Orleans, to report to the *LST 698* when it arrived from the shipyard in Jeffersonville, Ind. Fran came with him to New Orleans, and they had a delayed honeymoon while waiting for the ship.

His part in the war? That's what this book is all about!

After the war, returning to his wife Fran in Wilmette, Ill., he saw their six-month-old son, William Ellis Haswell, for the first time. Soon they added a daughter, Anne Loomis Haswell, and two more sons, Thomas Clayton and James Carson Haswell.

Haswell switched to public relations and for many years edited a large-circulation company publication. He was an accredited member of the Public Relations Society of America and retired in 1985.

In 1949 the couple bought their first home in northwest Evanston, Ill., and have lived in this area ever since.

Major interests over the years have been their four children and six grandchildren, their church and community activities. Haswell was involved for three decades in the Evanston 4th of July Association. Over a long period he and Fran have studied their family roots, visiting many libraries and cemeteries. He has done considerable writing and photography. Other interests include history, music enjoyment (classical to big band), and domestic and European travel.

Eventually, they retrieved from the attic the World War II letters he had written to Fran from overseas. These became the basis for the dozens of little happenings recorded in these pages.

For the past ten years, they have lived in a retirement community in Evanston, along with many other World War II veterans and spouses.

But they have not forgotten the thousands who never came back— and the parents, wives, and children who waited for them in vain. "*We were the lucky ones*," Haswell remarked.

Index of Places

(World War II Names)

(Omitting home cities of officers and men)

Admiralty Islands 40, 41, 110, 117, 208, 209, 224

Alaska 14

Aleutian Islands 181, 227

Ambridge, Pa. 206

Apo Island, Philippines 105

Arawe, New Britain 49

Attu, Aleutian Is., Alaska 15

Barbers Point, Oahu, T.H. 185

Biak, Schouten Islands xix, 17, 41, 66, 67, 68, 97, 126, 209, 213

Bikini Atoll, Marshall Islands 171

Bohol, Philippines 96, 107 (Sea)

Borneo, Dutch East Indies 13, 56, 85

Bosnik, Biak, Schouten Islands 67

Boston, Mass. (Harbor) 25 (Harbor), 206 (Navy Yard)

Bougainville, Solomon Islands 13, 27

Brunei, North Borneo, Dutch East Indies 13

Bungo Suido (Strait), Japan 148

Cape Engaño, Philippines 56

Cape Gloucester, New Britain 17, 41

Cape Horn, Chile 25

Caribbean Sea 26, 183

Caroline Islands 8, 16, 17, 39, 128, 168, 210, 213, 224

Catmon Hill 47, 69

Chesapeake Bay, Md. xix, 4

Chicago, Ill. 59, 67, 79, 88, 158, 189, 195, 196, 206, 230

China 8, 96 (South China Sea), 98, 102, 103, 147 (East China Sea)

Coco Solo, Panama Canal Zone 23 (Naval base), 207, 208

Colon Harbor, Panama Canal Zone 25

Coral Sea 13

Cristobal, Panama Canal Zone 7, 23

Cuba 14, 22, 207

Culebra Cut (Gaillard Cut), Panama Canal Zone 26

Columbia Lightship 189

Columbia River 189, 190, 192, 198

Davao, Philippines 9

Diamond Head, Oahu, T.H. 183, 231

Dinagat, island at entrance to Leyte Gulf, Philippines 45, 46, 55, 70, 96

Dulag, Leyte, Philippines viii, 40, 45, 46, 53, 208

Dutch East Indies 11, 13

Dutch Harbor, Alaska 14

Dutch New Guinea 17, 208, 209

Eniwetok Atoll, Marshall Islands xvii, xx, 17, 32, 34, 36, 37, 38, 40, 43, 83, 126, 130, 169, 171, 178, 208, 210, 211

Evanston, Ill. viii, 121, 231

Evansville, Ind. 204, 206

Finschhafen, Northeast New Guinea 17, 74, 77, 78, 81, 83, 87, 126, 209

Florida Island, Solomon Islands 117, 118, 119, 120, 121, 125, 126, 130, 210, 213

Formosa (Taiwan) 8, 133

Gaillard Cut (Culebra Cut), Panama Canal Zone 26

Gatun Lake, Panama Canal Zone 25 (Locks), 26

Gilbert Islands 11, 17, 227

Great Lakes, Ill. 1, 181, 197, 205, 230

Guadalcanal, Solomon Islands xiv, xix, xxviii, 11, 14, 15, 16, 18, 32, 114, 116, 117, 118, 119, 120, 122, 124, 125, 126, 127, 133, 134, 141, 155, 183

Guam, Mariana Islands 8, 9, 11, 17, 41, 98, 128, 156, 164

Guantanamo Bay, Cuba 19, 22, 207

Gulf of California, Mexico 24, 27

Gulf of Mexico 20

Gulfport, Miss. 4, 7, 207, 212

Halmahera, Dutch East Indies 85, 86

Hawaii, a U.S. territory 9, 14, 25, 29, 31, 38, 40, 67, 98, 155, 177, 178, 180, 181, 182, 208, 211

Hiroshima, Honshu, Japan 185, 186, 200, 202, 203, 226, 227

Hollandia, Dutch New Guinea 13, 15, 17, 40, 41, 43, 53, 58, 60, 62, 66, 68, 70, 71, 74, 80, 95, 97, 126, 134, 153, 178, 208, 209, 214, 219

Homonhon, island at entrance to Leyte Gulf, Philippines 45, 46, 96

Hong Kong 8, 11

Honolulu, Oahu, T.H. 31, 36, 83, 113, 178, 180, 181, 182

Humboldt Bay, Hollandia, Dutch New Guinea 60, 63, 73, 74, 77, 208, 209

Illinois xxvii, 83, 205, 206, 228

Ironbottom Sound, Guadalcanal, Solomon Islands 117, 118, 119, 120, 125

Iwo Jima 17, 149, 162

Japan xiv, xv, 8, 9, 10, 11, 12, 13, 14, 15, 16, 38, 39, 43, 55, 56, 57, 63, 64, 66, 67, 69, 70, 72, 75, 87, 94, 95, 96, 98, 99, 101, 109, 110, 119, 120, 127, 134, 136, 141, 142, 144, 147, 148, 149, 150, 152, 153, 160, 162, 164, 178, 186, 189, 200, 201, 202, 203, 226, 228

Java, Dutch East Indies 13

Jeffersonville, Ind. xxx, 1, 4, 204, 206, 230

Kadena, Okinawa 141

Kahoolawe, Maui, T.H. 32

Kailua, Oahu, T.H. 32, 183

Kaneohe Bay, Oahu, T.H. 10 (Naval Station), 32, 208, 212

Keawakapu, Maui, T.H. 32, 212

Kerama Retto, Okinawa Gunto, Ryukyu Islands ix, 133, 136, 137, 138, 150, 152, 153

Kiriwina, Milne Bay, Alaska 17

Kiska, Aleutian Is., Alaska 13

Koko Head, Oahu, T.H. 32, 212

Kwajalein Atoll, Marshall Islands 9, 17, 32, 41, 83, 178

Kukum Beach, Guadalcanal 125

Kyushu, Japan 127, 133, 201

Lae, Northeast New Guinea 13, 17, 41, 78

Lanai, Maui, T.H. 32

Leyte Gulf, Philippines 40, 44, 45, 46, 47, 53, 55, 56, 57, 58, 59, 68, 69, 70, 94, 96, 103, 107, 228

Leyte, Philippines 33, 38, 39, 40, 41, 42, 43, 44, 53, 54, 55, 56, 57, 59, 66, 69, 71, 86, 94, 96, 97, 101, 107, 110, 112, 119, 120, 126, 134, 145, 178, 183, 186, 208, 209, 212, 213, 219, 223, 224, 227, 228

Limon Bay, Panama Canal Zone 24, 25

Lingayen Gulf, Philippines ix, xiv, xix, 40, 89, 93, 94, 95, 97, 99, 100, 101, 102, 103, 107, 118, 126, 209, 223, 224

Lingayen, Luzon, Philippines 70, 91, 95, 96, 98, 102, 107, 114, 120, 124, 134, 183, 186, 213, 224

Lingga Roads, Singapore 55

London, England 38

Los Negros, Admiralty Islands 17, 41, 43

Luzon, Philippines 38, 56, 57, 89, 93, 94, 95, 96, 97, 98, 101, 112, 209, 213, 223, 224, 227

Maalaea Bay, Maui, T.H. 32 (Bay), 212

Madison, Wis. vii, 74, 121, 196, 230

Manchuria 8

Manila, Luzon, Philippines 91, 94, 95, 134, 144, 223

Manus, Admiralty Islands xix, 17, 34, 36, 38, 40, 41, 43, 60, 92, 97, 110, 111, 112, 113, 114, 115, 117, 123, 124, 133, 134, 153, 156, 158, 183, 208, 209, 210, 224

Marshall Islands 8, 17, 34, 98, 171, 208, 210, 224, 227

Maui, T.H. 29, 32, 208, 212

Maunalua Bay, Oahu, T.H. 32, 212

Merope Rock, Philippines 105

Midway Island 13, 14

Mindanao, Philippines 39, 55, 57, 96, 101, 107, 227

Mindanao Sea 96

Mindoro, Philippines 94, 96, 103, 104, 223

Mindoro Strait 103

Mios Woendi Lagoon, Palaido Is., Schouten Islands 67, 68, 209

Miraflores Locks, Panama Canal Zone 26

Mogmog Island, Ulithi 131, 155, 157, 160

Morotai, Netherlands East Indies xix, 17, 39, 41, 81, 82, 83, 85, 86, 87, 89, 90, 95, 97, 126, 209, 213

Mount Shuri, Okinawa 141, 142

Mount Surabachi, Okinawa 162

Nagasaki, Kyushu, Japan 185, 186, 200, 202

Nansei Shoto, Okinawa Jima 151, 224

Negros, Panay Is., Philippines 96

Netherlands East Indies 17, 60, 81, 82, 85, 208, 209

New Guinea xix, 11, 13, 17, 36, 40, 41, 53, 58, 60, 63, 66, 70, 74, 77, 78, 82, 98, 117, 227

New Orleans, La. xvii, xix, 1, 2, 3, 4, 6, 7, 19, 29, 47, 61, 112, 196, 204, 207, 212, 219, 230

Noemfoor, Dutch New Guinea 17, 95

Normandy 39

Noumea, New Caledonia 126

Oahu, T. H. 32, 92, 182, 185, 208, 211, 212, 213

Okinawa Gunto (archipelago), Ryukyu Islands ix, xiii, xiv, xv, xvii, xix, xx, 40, 119, 125, 127, 127, 131, 133, 134, 135, 136, 137, 138, 139, 140, 141, 142, 143, 148, 149, 150, 151, 162, 165, 168, 186, 210, 213, 223, 225, 227, 228

Okinawa Jima (island) 210, 220, 224

Ormoc, Leyte, Philippines 94

Oro Bay 95

Pacific Ocean 27, 36, 224

Palau Islands 224

Panama Canal xiv, xvii, 8, 19, 22, 24, 25, 28, 207, 208, 226

Panama City, Fla. 4, 5, 6, 7, 27, 76, 207

Papua New Guinea 14, 209

Pearl Harbor, Oahu, T.H. 31, 32, 34, 35, 38, 43, 60, 83, 121, 128, 153, 155, 160, 161, 162, 166, 169, 170, 171, 172, 177, 178, 181, 184, 185, 198, 208, 211, 212, 214, 219, 226, 227

Pedro Miguel Locks, Panama Canal Zone 26

Peleliu, Palau Islands 39, 149

Philippines ix, xvii, xix, 8, 11, 38, 39, 40, 43, 44, 55, 56, 57, 67, 68, 70, 78, 80, 83, 93, 94, 95, 96, 97,

98, 101, 102, 103, 104, 109, 126, 133, 134, 147, 154, 208, 209, 212, 213, 224, 225, 227

Pittsburgh, Pa. 26, 206

Portland, Ore. xvii, xix, xx, 185, 186, 188, 189, 191, 195, 197, 198, 211

Port Moresby, Papua New Guinea 13, 14

Port Purvis, Florida Island 117, 118, 125, 126, 210

Puget Sound, Wash. 184, 185, 186

Quebec, Canada 38, 39

Rabaul, New Britain, Bismark Archipelago 11, 13, 16, 43

Ryukyu Islands, Japanese Archipelago 148, 210, 213

Saidor, New Guinea 17

Saipan, Mariana Islands 17, 31, 32, 41, 83, 98, 162, 178

Samar Island, Philippines 56, 107, 110, 223

San Bernardino Strait, Philippines 55

San Diego, Calif. xvii, 27, 28 (Naval Base), 29, 36, 59, 198, 208

San Francisco, Calif. 25, 123, 134, 136, 156

San Pedro Bay, Philippines 40, 46, 66, 69, 103, 107, 110, 223

Sansapor, Dutch New Guinea 17, 95

Santiago, Cuba 22

Sarangani Bay, Mindanao, Philippines 39

Savo Island, Solomon Islands 118, 119

Schenectady, N.Y. 26

Schouten Islands 17, 66, 209, 213

Seattle, Wash. 197, 198

Seeadler Harbor, Manus 34, 37, 43, 112 (Bay), 114, 115, 117 (Bay), 208, 210

Seneca, Ill. xxvii, 206, 228

Sibuyan Sea, Philippines 55

Singapore 9, 11, 13, 55, 57

Solomon Islands 11, 13, 14, 117, 119, 210, 213

Sulu Sea, Philippines 96

Surigao Strait, Philippines 55, 96, 107, 223

Sydney, Australia 126, 127, 192

Tacloban, Leyte, Philippines viii, 40, 53, 97, 103, 107, 108, 109, 110

Taiwan (Formosa) 8, 38, 101, 133

Tanamerah Bay 60

Tarawa Atoll, Gilbert Islands 17, 32, 149

Tillamook Light Rock 189

Timor, New Guinea 11, 13

Tinian, Mariana Islands 32

Tokyo Bay, Japan xiii, 9, 10, 12, 18, 136, 226

Truk, Caroline Islands 16, 186

Tulagi Island, Solomon Islands xix, 13, 14, 32, 118, 126, 127, 133

Ulithi Atoll, Caroline Islands 17, 39, 127, 128, 130, 133, 134, 152, 153, 155, 156, 157, 164, 166, 178, 183, 210, 213

Waikiki, Honolulu, Hawaii 31, 180, 181, 182

Wakde, Dutch New Guinea' 17
Wake Island (U.S.) 9, 11
Wilmette, Ill. 1, 3, 73, 196, 230
Willamette River 189
Woodlark Island, Milne Bay 17
Yap, Caroline Islands 32, 34, 35,
    37, 38, 39, 40, 41, 128
Zampa Misaki, Okinawa 143, 147

BVG